# *Thrive!*

"Felicia Scott is a gifted young woman who has embraced her own personal challenges to experience transformation, empowerment and change. She is a strong and solid voice to her generation." —Pastor Jacqueline McCullough

"There is nothing ordinary about Felicia Scott or [*Thrive!*] — finally the invisible...woman can be seen."
—Dr. Bertice Berry, bestselling author and lecturer

"Felicia has an extraordinary way with words. Reading this book spiritually inspires me to delve into my own life experiences in order to understand who I am, who I was and who I ultimately would like to be." —Cheryl James-Wray "Salt" from "Salt-N-Pepa"

"If you want to feel inspired, encouraged and ready to tell your enemies to "bring it on"...you must pick up this book."
—Rev. Elizabeth Rios, M.A.
Founder, Center for Emerging Female Leadership

"*Thrive!* is a divine encounter for the 21st Century godly woman to be able to flourish inspite of her past issues. As always, Scott is keeping it real by bringing practical solutions to the ordinary woman that will propel her into extraordinary living."
—Min. Ruth Fitzgerald cofounder, Wake-Up Ministry

"[*Thrive!*] takes readers on a journey through...moments of uncertainty, through various stages of self-awareness and ultimately discovering life's universal truths."—*Black Issues Book Review*

"[*Thrive!*] connects with everyone and offers...both spiritual renewal and self-empowerment to overcome the past and design a future that will bring fulfillment, peace, joy, and all the other things that make life worth living." —*Black Elegance*

BUTTERFLY
WORKS

Teaching · Touching · Transforming

www.butterflyworks.net

# Thrive!

## 7 Strategies
## for Extraordinary Living

## Felicia T. Scott

For information, contact:
Butterfly Works, P.O. Box 5434, New York, NY 10185
The purpose of this book is to educate, encourage and
inspire the reader. The author and Butterfly Works shall
have neither liability nor responsibility to any person or
entity with respect to any loss or damage, caused or alleged
to be caused, directly or indirectly by the information
contained in this book.

Publisher: Butterfly Works, New York, NY
http://www.butterflyworks.net
Cover Design: Allison Warner
Book Interior Design & Layout: Scott Osborne
Editor: Deborah Cowell
Proofreader: Fernando Gomez
Printed in the United States of America

ISBN 0-9704898-1-1
1. Inspirational
2. Personal Development/Growth
3. Self-Help

*Thrive!*

---

7 Strategies
for Extraordinary Living

---

*by*

Felicia T. Scott

*Thrive! 7 Strategies for Extraordinary Living* is the revised and expanded version of the book formerly titled *From My Window: Relevant Expressions of an Ordinary Woman*. My sincerest thanks to those of you who supported *From My Window*. Your invaluable insights provided during our H.E.A.L.I.N.G.™ Journey seminars, talks, book parties and e-mails helped this work evolve into a personal transformation tool that I believe will encourage and inspire you to make your life extraordinary!

This book is dedicated
to the memory of my father,
the late Willie James Scott,
and my mother, Ezzie B. Scott.

To Daddy,
You will always be my Prince.
The memory of your smile is now
and forever will be the sweetest part of life.
I will love and miss you always!

To Mama,
You are the song that sings
in every season of my life.
Thank you for being a woman of
tremendous courage, incredible strength,
dignity and grace.
*I love you!*

July 3, 1998

Dear Lord,

As I sit here today, my prayer is that you will turn every pain I've ever experienced into a powerful written word that will transform someone else's life. I pray that you will turn every tear into a reservoir of wisdom from which others can drink and be satisfied. Lord, turn the crumbs of small thoughts into the bread of greatness. Turn every moment of loneliness into a place where I can learn the beauty of solitude and communion with you. Turn every question into a steadfast faith. Turn every disappointment into an unexpected victory. Lord, take my life and turn it into a testimony.

Sincerely,

Felicia T. Scott
Encouragement Coach

# Contents

## PART ONE

# Contents

# PART TWO

## THRIVE! H.E.A.L.I.N.G.™ JOURNALING GUIDE

# Foreword

The greatest challenge with life is that it's daily. We must face each day with its uncertainties, disappointments, failures, regrets and frustrations, along with its opportunities, possibilities and hopes. For many, living can be more difficult than death. I have always said, "The greatest tragedy in life is not death, but rather life without a sense of purpose."

Being born into the human race qualifies you for the hurts, joys, changes, needs and growth processes that life demands. However, successful passage through the uncharted waters of life's ocean is only possible with the compass of a *sense of divine purpose and destiny*. After all, it is not what happens to you that really matters, but what you do about what happens. In essence, your response to life is more important than what life throws your way.

Few individuals have mastered the secrets to overcoming the challenges of life. The key to effective living is learning the principles and precepts established by the Creator. Felicia T. Scott has captured these time-tested principles and precepts in her masterful work, *Thrive! 7 Strategies for Extraordinary Living*. Her experiences, which are common to us all, serve as the backdrop for her lessons and strategies that are both human and divine.

This book is a classic presentation of the eternal wisdom embedded in the knowledge of God and His love for mankind. Her simple approach leaves a profound impact on the human spirit. Her skill with a poet's pen composes each line into a musical tune that makes the heart sing, cry, smile and think. I love this work and encourage you to read it with an open heart and mind.

*Thrive!* will help you strive for the best in life and give you the tools to overcome all obstacles. Read on, explore and enjoy its timeless wisdom!

Great work!

Dr. Myles E. Munroe
BFM International
Nassau, Bahamas

# Introduction

In light of the heightened interest of the need for "spirit" care, many books have been written to help us deal with the emotional side of life that is often overlooked or completely ignored. Unfortunately, most people feel distanced from or embarrassed by the sometimes elusive and cerebral theories that encourage us to discover the "inner child" or "embrace the real self." Ordinary people have difficulty connecting with such abstract terminology and shy away from psychological terms or concepts that must be explained by trained experts.

Before I continue, I wish to clearly state that I am a supporter of mental health counseling and fully recognize its benefits. In fact, I believe there are many cases in which professional help must be used to make any real or tangible breakthroughs. However, one thing remains true of the person seeking professional help or just trying to understand himself or herself better — you are the author of your own destiny! Healing can only take place if you are ready and willing to face the issues of your life and make the necessary changes. Dealing with the complexities of human emotions is not easy. Like physical health, emotional health takes time, exercise and discipline. But its rewards include more fulfilling relationships and a well-rounded life.

Your relationship with yourself is second only to a relationship with God. The idea of a relationship with yourself is foreign to many. We just don't make the time for spiritual connection to our true emotions and philosophies. We live our lives out of necessity, disconnected from our real desires, hopes and fears. Most of our actions are dictated by "need to," leaving very little time for self-discovery. Neglecting yourself is dangerous and it cheats every single relationship that you have in your life.

**THRIVE!** The word alone has the power to make you feel like you can take on the world. And you can, but let's be real, shall we? This book will not change your life overnight. It will not solve all of your problems. All of the answers you need for a successful life are not in this one book. Promising you attractive results without focusing on the effort you will have to invest in your own transformation is the stuff fantasies are made of. Your transformation won't take place until your actions and thoughts about life begin to change.

However, with the strategies discussed in this book, I believe you can begin to resolve some of the issues in your life. You will be inspired and encouraged to take an honest assessment of your thoughts and attitudes, and then challenged to take some practical steps toward improving yourself and your life. Extraordinary living is not problem-free living. It is living in emotional and spiritual control of your reactions to the challenges of life.

This book is about personal evolution through H.E.A.L.I.N.G.™ Originally titled *From My Window: Relevant Expressions of an Ordinary Woman*, it was self-published in the New York area in the fall of 2001, shortly after the tragic events of September 11. As I traveled around the country sharing the book's message, I became keenly aware of the great need for H.E.A.L.I.N.G.™ in individuals and communities.

My original mission with *From My Window* was to share with others the lessons I learned as I overcame depression. Having suffered in silence for seven years myself, I was aware of the fact that many people suffer from depression in isolation without the support of family and friends. However, I quickly realized that beyond depression, many people just needed encouragement in dealing with the daily stresses of family, work and society that often stretch us and in their own way breed dysfunctions as we try to fit into the different roles that we have chosen or have been forced into. In response, the work evolved into a personal transformation tool purposed to encourage and inspire you to "make your life extraordinary." This expanded and revised edition also features the **Thrive! H.E.A.L.I.N.G.™ Journaling Guide** to help you apply the lessons of self-discovery you will learn.

It is time for you to realize that you control your destiny. You can live an extraordinary life! You can live free from the weight of your past. You can find the courage to live your dreams. Every task can be mastered if approached with a sound and reasonable plan, some flexibility and a resolve to win. God ultimately has the best in mind for all of us, but we must assert our rights to extraordinary living! Life will provide the opportunities, but we must do the work of seizing them by finding our seat in the classroom of life.

*Thrive!* is about your journey. It is about moving beyond the realm of merely surviving into a life that is full and satisfying. You have been through so many challenges already. You've already faced situations beyond your imagination — you know that you can survive. But are you ready to do more? Are you ready to define success and personal fulfillment for yourself? Are you ready to Thrive?

First, a disclaimer: I do not declare myself to be an expert on anything or anyone other than myself. I am a woman who battled depression for seven years. I spent my late teens and early adulthood in an emotional vacuum, void of hope and self-love. I am sharing these lessons as a friend who seeks to encourage you to do whatever it takes for your emotional health and well-being. On my journey of H.E.A.L.I.N.G.™, I discovered seven strategies for extraordinary living. They are:

*H.* Help While You're Hurting
*E.* Enjoy Life's Process
*A.* Accept and Anticipate Change
*L.* Let Go...
*I.* Itemize Your Issues and Images
*N.* Navigate Your Needs
*G.* Grow with Gratitude

## OVERVIEW OF THE STRATEGIES

**Help While You're Hurting** — Though it seems like a contradiction to help someone while you're in pain, the truth is that you can't sit around just waiting to feel better about your life. Your productivity, IN SPITE OF your pain is the key to your freedom. Your healing will come from exercising your muscles and using whatever strength you already possess. You don't need more; you just need to do something with what you already have!

**Enjoy Life's Process** — Find the blessings of where you currently are and you will unleash a power in your life that will help you convert adversity into wisdom. Your current obstacle is an opportunity for character development. Stop focusing on the destination and the spot somewhere down the road — enjoy the journey right where you are!

**Accept and Anticipate Change** — Change is inevitable. Don't waste your strength fighting it; learn to accept change as a part of your life. You will never know peace until you learn to accept things beyond your control and work with the things within your circle of influence. You'll soon realize that change is your friend and instead of dreading its visit — you'll anticipate its coming.

**Let Go...** — You can't get to the second floor without leaving the first! It is just that simple. Some of your heart's desires cannot come to you until you let go of the things, people, images and thought patterns that you find your identity and security in. Letting go can feel like losing — but that is far from the truth. You'll soon see that you're not losing; you are just making room!

**Itemize Your Issues and Images** — Stop giving your life a superficial glance. You need to head the inspection team on the search for undisclosed weapons of mass destruction in your emotions and thought life. No offense, but you've got issues. We all do. But in order to Thrive! you must know what's stopping you on the inside. Once you discover your internal boundaries, nothing on the outside will be able to hinder your progress and success.

**Navigate Your Needs** — Our lives are constructed around our needs. We work to provide food and shelter. We engage in relationships to meet our need for emotional expression. Get in touch with your emotional and spiritual needs because, whether you realize it or not, they are driving you! You can take the driver's seat once you identify what your needs are!

**Grow with Gratitude** — Balance is the key to successful living. Know your needs, but get in touch with your God-given abilities that have helped you every step of the way. True gratitude produces instant results in our minds, bodies and spirits.

*H:* **Help While You're Hurting**

*E:* Enjoy Life's Process

*A:* Accept and Anticipate Change

*L:* Let Go...

*I:* Itemize Your Issues and Images

*N:* Navigate Your Needs

*G:* Grow with Gratitude

# STRATEGY ONE

*Help While You're Hurting*

Productivity in spite of the pain is the aim of this strategy. Like Olympic athletes who perform despite their injuries, we must continue to function in the face of our pains. The denial of pain only serves to dilute reality, but a vision for the pain enables us to Thrive! Learn to take your experiences and transform them into wisdom that can be shared with others. Despite your heartache, you must be willing to invest your life in the success of others. Opportunities abound to put this strategy into practice. If you're feeling lonely, don't lock yourself in the house with a pint of ice cream and an old movie. Invite someone out to dinner who you know is going through a difficult time. Quiet the raging of your own heart by being a sounding board for someone else. Listening to others' problems broadens our perspective and lessens the feelings of isolation that we often experience when going through difficult times.

Helping others can take our minds off our own problems and give us a much-needed break. This break is not an escape, but rather a time to refresh that enables us to approach our challenges with renewed vision. Helping others is a proclamation of faith in God's faithfulness and your resilience. Our emotional stinginess sometimes "blocks our blessings" and the blessings of those around us. We refuse to share our experience; meanwhile others have gone through or are going through the exact same thing. Serving others sets the stage for our come back. Helping someone is a natural elixir. Give yourself a daily dose. It can start out small, but it will grow. And as you participate in the H.E.A.L.I.N.G.™ journey of others, it will reassure you of your own strength and purpose.

> "IF WE FAIL TO DEFINE THE ROLE PAIN
> WILL PLAY IN OUR LIVES, THE PAIN WILL
> REDEFINE US IN ITS IMAGE."

## CHAPTER I
## OPPORTUNITY OR OBSTACLE?

Pain makes you feel singled out. Though you know you're not the only person experiencing pain, you somehow feel as if you are alone to face it. That is because when pain touches your life, it touches your uniqueness. Don't be alarmed by its arrival, the fact that you are experiencing pain is just an indicator of your humanity. Pain isn't picking on you. In fact, pain isn't prejudiced and doesn't hold any biases. Regardless of who you are, regardless of your economic status, regardless of your race — pain will touch you. It is the only real equal-opportunity employer.

So, what do you do with pain? The first thing you have to do is define it. You can define it as "something I will never, ever get over," or you can define it as "an opportunity for growth and development." It is up to you. Torrential rains fall on the rich and poor man's harvest alike. The poor man weeps as he watches what the rain has destroyed. The rich man goes out into the fields to see what can be salvaged. If nothing can be salvaged, he plants a crop that can thrive in the new conditions.

When hit with hard times, our immediate response is to focus on the unfairness of it. This attitude is nonproductive and only serves to send your mind and emotions into a tailspin. If you've let yourself go there — stop! Take your power back! You can't change what has already happened to you. You just have to be smart enough to know how to work with it and get the most out of it. You're not cursed. You're just going through the process of living and that involves some pain. And like it or not, it will probably be the very thing that will make you a better friend, listener and person. People who have experienced pain and dealt with it from a healthy perspective tend to be more sensitive to others and can connect on levels of intimacy that only come from experience.

## DEFINING MOMENTS

If you fail to define your pain, you will spend the rest of your life allowing it to define you. Pain will not restrict itself to your immediate experience. Instead it will travel through time, forging a connection between the past and the future. Unless you deal with the effects of being in an abusive relationship, you will hear the negative voice of the past even though the promise of the present is speaking. The stench of pain from the past can overwhelm the fragrance of new love and possibility.

People who fail to deal with their pain live in a defensive mode — constantly on guard as they wait for the next disappointment. They are acutely aware of their own sensitivities and pains, but oblivious to those hurting around them. Quite often, their unresolved bitterness and anger becomes a source of abuse to others.

Pain distorts our emotional vision and impairs our ability to properly understand the situations of our lives. Pain is so powerful that it can feed the mind thoughts of fear that have no root in reality, but nevertheless paralyze our emotions. How many times have you cried after a fresh break-up? Your emotions were crushed, not only for the loss of the current relationship, but somewhere deep inside fear whispered that love would never find you again. It wasn't true and isn't true, but until you are stronger than the moment, you can't expect anything from the future.

I wear eyeglasses and when I remove them my vision becomes blurry. Nothing is distinguishable and everything runs together. Pain affects our emotional senses in much of the same way. It hinders our ability to see life and people as they truly are by causing us to question our own value and worth. You can even lose sight of yourself — the most important person in your life! Decisions made in a pained state of mind are usually poorly thought out and hazardous. They can put your spiritual, emotional and physical life in jeopardy.

## WHIP IT INTO SHAPE!

The most important thing that you must remember as you wrestle with the onslaught of pain is that it is usually temporary. Even if the pain is caused by something like the death of a loved one, your strength to manage it will increase as you face it. Pain struts onto the center stage of your life and tells you that you will never love again, trust again, be happy again or be the same again. Remind your pain that you are the author of your destiny. It has a role to play, but it won't be the star of your life's show!

The only way to direct the show of your life is to get a vision for your pain. You cannot allow pain to come into your life without determining that it will somehow benefit you. You must decide to find opportunity in everything! If you are in financial pain due to poor decisions, and now face the effects of negative credit and the shame of poor financial management, you can either hang your head down or you can get up, get a budget and get about the business of restoring your life. It will take time and effort, but you can do it. If you have lost a loved one, don't dishonor their memory by shutting others out. Instead, spread the love and the lessons given to you by sharing with others.

Discipline is required to see the fulfillment of vision. Focusing on the bigger picture helps you to push beyond the current pain. I once worked with a personal fitness trainer. Having exhausted all my excuses as to why I couldn't fit my clothes, I had to face reality. My clothes weren't shrinking — I was expanding. On Mondays and Wednesdays, I disliked my trainer — not because of the person, but because of his mission. He pushed me beyond my limits — actually beyond my *perceived* limits. He forced me to dig deeper and discover strength and muscles that I didn't even know existed. It hurt, but I saw results. You will see results if you don't give in to the pain. There is more to you than you've discovered and the only way it will be revealed is through adversity. But the strength and power are there — the challenge only exposes who you really are!

## **Blur**

Without my glasses,
It's all a blur.
Things are fuzzy and I can't really see.

I can see dimly,
And some things I can associate with,
But still I cannot truly see.

Colors have lost their sharpness,
As life has lost its clarity.
I want to make sense of some things,
Some feelings, some emotions.

Everything runs together,
Because without my glasses
I can't really appreciate the beauty of a print
Woven by love.

I can't really see what I'm looking at,
Everything is a strain.

Lord, be my glasses.
Help me to clearly see,
Everything that has become muddied
And blurred by pain.

> "THE PAIN LETS YOU KNOW
> THAT YOU ARE STILL ALIVE!"

## CHAPTER 2
## TELL IT LIKE IT IS

It's not happiness. It's not sorrow. It's not hope. It is not despair. The danger of ignoring what pain is telling us is the numbness that results from denial.

Though pain is uncomfortable and challenging to the spirit, it alerts you to your issues. Like a toothache or discomfort in the body, pain may be signaling that deeper issues need to be addressed. Numbness blocks the message pain is sending to our bodies and, like an undetected cancer, emotional issues may be festering in our hearts while ravaging our spirits and damaging our relationships.

You have convinced yourself that you're okay and that what happened meant nothing to you. But deep down inside, you know something is wrong. You know the incident has left its imprint in your emotions. The fact that you aren't hurting any more has deceived you, and you have managed to make yourself and others believe that you are actually recovering. Are you fooling yourself? Are you really healed or are you just desensitized?

## EMOTIONAL NARCOTICS

Pain and disappointment work together to form the powerful narcotic of numbness. It produces a false sense of reality and creates a detached awareness from our surroundings. It dopes the emotions into silence and causes the mind to draw a blank over the offenses. You are in a self-preservation mode that is leading you into more danger than what you are struggling to protect yourself from.

Emotions are the seasonings of life. Is there anything that feels better than love? Our ability to experience sensations in our spirit is priceless. Even negative emotions can be used to our advantage when we examine them to gain a greater understanding of our thought processes. But like everything else, when our emotions go unchecked and are allowed to dictate our actions outside of the parameters of reason — we are in danger! Despite how dangerous it can be to lose emotional control, there is one thing more dangerous than this — it is the denial of our emotions. Nothing has a more destructive effect on your emotional and spiritual health than your refusal to face your emotions. In order to deal with them you will create a false reality that keeps you from facing the truth.

Your refusal to face the truth will negatively impact all areas of your life.

## THE TRUTH THAT FREES

A friend of mine used to complain that she didn't feel part of her own family. Though she knew they loved her and that she loved them, she felt that they did not understand her. Upon getting to know my friend and her family more closely, I quickly realized that the problem wasn't her family but her refusal to deal with her past. A victim of sexual abuse as a child, she was angry at the loss of her innocence and believed her parents had failed to do everything they could to protect her. As the oldest child, she resented her younger sisters and brothers. Her anger at the abuse and the abuser was transferred to them. She resented any interest her parents showed in her siblings, and viewed it as favoritism. While she had diagnosed her family as being the problem, her bitterness over her childhood was the real issue. Her negativity distanced her from her siblings as they sensed her resentfulness, and they shied away from developing an intimate relationship with her. Without knowing it, she was abusive and critical towards those she loved most. Until she was ready to deal with the "real" problem, she was unable to enjoy healthy relationships. Only the truth could restore her life. The truth you know and acknowledge is the key to your liberation and emotional freedom.

H.E.A.L.I.N.G.™ can't come until you acknowledge your present condition and locate the source of your emotions. True personal change begins when we become ruthless in digging up the truth about ourselves. It transcends your personal experience, when you are able to share your lessons openly with others without fear.

Life is limited when you allow negative experiences to permanently alter your perception of life's possibilities. Wisdom dictates that our experiences are commas in the sentence of life — meaning more can come after them. The story can take on a new direction. You have stunted yourself when you let your negative experience become a period — you've closed the door on something new.

## NO EXCUSES

Sometimes our emotions can take a lesson from the physically challenged. They learn how to live despite their disabilities. When we are temporarily handicapped emotionally, we must learn to live in control of our condition. Sometimes we just can't spring back immediately, but we must never become "used to" being emotionally disabled.

We can't use excuses, because life doesn't accept excuses. Life responds to persistence. There are no magic cures and sometimes you just have to do it. I can't tell you how to muster up the "feelings" to get the job done. Just do it even though you don't feel it — the emotions will soon follow suit. Whatever you're afraid to face, force yourself to face it. Hiding from it doesn't make it go away. Hiding only serves to make its effects last even longer.

## n u m b

numb
numb...

frozen in a moment
in a place in time.
my past and future
playing before me.

everything is in motion,
yet i am sadly still.
living in a limbo that i don't understand.

aware of the changes before me
knowing they are "the inevitable."
nevertheless, i fight them
i struggle...

trapped in the questions
for which others lack answers.
waiting for my body and mind
to line up with my heart.

everything i do and feel
seems to be standing outside of the real me.
like a robot, programmed to "just dealing."
what about overcoming?

mustering strength for every move
don't take my smile for granted,
because it took everything in me to paint it for you.

please let me make you laugh,
because only then do i know that i can
touch someone else.

numb...
numb...
encased in ice.

reality, rehearsal
truth, fiction
who do you see?
the image i've perfected, or
do you really see me?

"i know you," you say
but how can that be?
for i've discovered sometimes i'm a stranger
not who i thought myself to be.

i'm just numb
but don't worry.
it will pass
i'll "live" again
i'll destroy the mask.

> "TO LIVE ONLY FOR YOURSELF IS TO MISS
> THE MEANING AND POWER OF LIFE."

CHAPTER 3
JUST WHAT THE DOCTOR ORDERED

Retreat and isolation tend to be our initial response to pain. Both physical and emotional attacks cause us to withdraw when we have been hurt, rejected or offended. Our emotional energies shut down, and we stagger in a state of inertia. We are hungry for companionship in our pain, yet we shy away from probing questions. We want comfort and reassurance, but to accept them would prove that something is really wrong. During these times we just want a break. Emotional pain can be physically fatiguing and it is natural to want to withdraw, but a healthy "time out" is different from throwing in the towel.

Helping someone else is one of the prescriptions for dealing with pain. By helping others and sharing your experience, you open your heart to new solutions and the answers needed for your own life are often discovered. Your self-esteem soars as you provide emotional comfort for someone else. Your actions serve as a reminder of your own strength and capabilities.

## WALKING BY FAITH

It is an expression of faith to invest your wisdom and emotions in others. Though you could forget the world and just focus on "self," you are subconsciously communicating a message of strength to your spirit. You are reminding yourself that the world is bigger than where you are, and if the world is bigger then you can move to a new and better place in it. In essence, you are recognizing that God has a purpose for your life, and by having faith you are declaring that He is bigger than your challenge. God always responds to faith.

Biblical wisdom inspires us to "fight the good fight of faith." Unleashing faith is a powerful exercise that makes demands on your expectations and perspective by requiring you to stretch to see the possibilities. You must dig deep within and meet negativity with faith in God's goodness. Never acting alone, faith will demand that you have hope and love in your heart. Defeat is a part of every success story. If hope is alive, then it's simply not over. Hope always finds a new way, a new perspective — hope just won't quit! Hope is more than the belief that things *can* change and become better — it is the expectancy that it *will* happen for you!

## THE GIFT THAT KEEPS ON GIVING

Sharing your experience with others is like winning a battle a thousand times over. When you first defeat it, it's for you. But as you share the experience with someone else, you encourage them and release hope into their lives. A word of caution however — be wise about who you share your heart with. Make sure you have the strength to face what others may try to do with your weaknesses. I have had the experience of sharing my weakness with individuals who could not handle

them and either distanced themselves from me, or used my
frailty as a weapon in a time of disagreement.

Once you've determined that you are ready — by all means
share! Help others avoid the same pitfalls. Let your experi-
ence be the foundation for others to make better decisions.
Get involved in the community and world around you. We
help others because each of us has something others can ben-
efit from. Again, you must use balance. Some people don't
want to change, and you must learn to walk away from anyone
who doesn't seem to want better for themselves. But foolish is
the person who walks away thinking that they have not been
impacted by someone else's failure. Everyone is needed and
no one can be replaced. We all lose out when those around us
fail to develop and reach their full potential. Controlling
others is not an option available to you. But by maximizing
your gifts and talents, you not only enrich your life — you
impact the lives of so many others. You must tell your story!

### It's On!

Equality, freedom and hope,
For the race known as man.
Humans of integrity,
Who fight and take a stand.
Not just for America,
But in each and every land.
Dream On, Martin!  Dream On!

Streets where peace and love,
Rule and reign every night.
Where you are really my brother
And concerned about my plight.

Hope for us all,
Be you yellow, red, black or white!
Right On, Malcolm!  Right On!

Running through the darkness,
Guided by freedom's light.
Knowing that you'll see tomorrow,
If you make it through tonight.
The law says you're wrong,
But God says you're right.
Once you taste of liberty —
Break bread, so that I too can bite!
Run On, Harriet!  Run On!

I am my brother's keeper,
In his fight he's not alone!
And though you call me free,
His chains are not his own.
To rest while he is struggling,
Is not righteous — It's just wrong.
Preach On, John Brown!  Preach On!

Not concerned about the people,
Just looking out for self.
Talking about democracy,
When what you really want is their wealth.
Ranking by priority —
My world first and yours comes third.
But even through all the lies,
The truth can still be heard!
Talk On, Biko!  Talk On!

Got your foot on your brother's neck.
Because his arms are still too weak.
But his heart is strong with courage,
Though you withhold that which he seeks.
And even though you hate him,
The voice of wisdom speaks,
Love On, Gandhi!  Love On!

Some of them were free men,
And some of them were slaves.
But they are true heroes
Whose sacrifices made the way.
Though their bodies are absent,
They still speak from the grave.
Saying Fight On, My Brothers!  Fight On!

Time to make the demand from "self,"
That we often make of others.
Take the mask off our faces,
So that truth can be uncovered.

When ready to make the change,
Reach up, for God's Spirit hovers.
Saying...
Dream On!  Write On!  Teach On!  Speak On!
Fight On!  Preach On!  Run On!  Love On!
Your time of serving ignorance is gone!
It's On, My People!  It's On!

*H:* Help While You're Hurting

**E: Enjoy Life's Process**

*A:* Accept and Anticipate Change

*L:* Let Go…

*I:* Itemize Your Issues and Images

*N:* Navigate Your Needs

*G:* Grow with Gratitude

# STRATEGY TWO

## Enjoy Life's Process

A "microwave mentality" can retard your growth. Although we live in the age of fast food, high-speed Internet access, and express checkout grocery lines, quality still comes through the process of time. Life won't give us everything on demand, and when it doesn't we must resist the urge to become bitter and frustrated. Instead we must learn to enjoy the moment we are in and bloom where we've been planted. Instead of hoping for the outside to change, we must focus on the controllable factor of changing on the inside. Setting goals and having dreams are necessary for motivation and focus, but we must balance our desires for the future with an appreciation of the gifts that life offers today. Own your life — moment by moment — because this moment is all you really have. You are hoping for a moment in the future, which, when it comes, will be called now.

> "NO PROGRESS
> WITHOUT PROCESS."

## CHAPTER 4
## WHAT'S COOKING?

### HOME-COOKED CHARACTER

We live in a microwave society. Quick and fast is how we like it. We hate waiting on lines, we don't like being put on hold, and for some strange reason, we don't like it when anything takes time. For evidence of this cultural philosophy, just look at the weight-loss industry. Year after year, billions of dollars are spent on products promising quick fixes for weight gain and obesity. Advertisers make claims that inches and pounds will be shed within days — healthily! You can have the body you want without any pain or discomfort. Just pop a pill and instantly, you can be on *Baywatch!* Absolute nonsense, right? Yet millions of intelligent people fall for these empty promises. Hard-earned money is wasted on fantasy pills that promise to reverse immediately in days and weeks what it took years to gain. We have forgotten that lasting results come through time and sacrifice. Anything worth having will require hard work.

## MY EVE-O-LUTION

At the age of 16 my life just seemed to "suddenly" go down-hill. I didn't understand it. I was an honors student who enjoyed learning, I was active in school activities and I loved spending time with my friends. I didn't know how to handle the damaging emotions and negative thoughts that began to consume my life. It seemed as if overnight everything ceased to matter. I remember being ashamed of my feelings. I had always thought that if external things were in order, then happiness would follow. I had good parents, enjoyed school and though I didn't have all the trappings of material success, I did enjoy a comfortable and stress-free life. My initial response to depression's assault was passive. I believed that it would just sort of go away and I'd wake up feeling better one day. I waited for that day for six years and nothing happened. Finally, it dawned on me. My depression wasn't sudden. It had been building over time. My healing would have to happen the same way, and I had an active role to play in the process.

For me, depression was the product of allowing negative words and thoughts to take root in my heart and mind. I allowed others to speak words into my life that caused me to question my own worth, validity and attractiveness. I was influenced by the images of those around me. I was never a small person and I was always bigger than my other friends. At age twelve while some still wore children's dresses, I was a size three in women's clothing. Now I know that a size three isn't big at all, but when everyone else is smaller you might as well be a size thirty-three. My physical flaws were magnified in my mind as I flipped through teen magazines filled with girls who didn't look anything like me. I made a judgment call against myself, without even knowing it. I decided that I just wasn't "enough."

## ELEVATE YOUR MIND!

I was looking for my circumstances to change in order to feel better about myself, but I actually needed to reprogram my thinking in order for change to take place. It wasn't a matter of losing weight, dating, or the host of other things that I once thought would bring contentment and satisfaction. It was about learning to be content with my life. It was about learning to love me for me. As long as I relied on circumstances to find happiness, my emotional liberation evaded me.

For me, the first step towards real recovery came through journaling and writing. In my own words, scripted by my hands, I began to see that the way I felt about myself was the root cause of my problems. I didn't like myself, and it wasn't because I wasn't acceptable. I didn't like myself because I'd allowed others to impose their standards of beauty, worth and success on me. I was giving others control of my life instead of accepting personal responsibility. While I do believe that depression can be biochemical, I firmly believe that a lot of depression is the result of unhealthy thinking and rejection of self. I realized that God had given me the power of choice. I had to choose to find meaning in my life and work through my pain. I had to actively seek out the resources and the people that could help me face the battle. As a sentence, it sounds so simple and easy, but as a process it took years for me to learn to love myself and appreciate my life.

There are no shortcuts when dealing with damaged emotions. There is no magical formula or one-time positive affirmation that will heal you. You must delve into your issues, honestly analyze them for what they are, then give it time. It is a process. It's days, weeks, months and sometimes years of believing and hoping, even when it appears to be hopeless.

## REWARDS

Fiery trials forge priceless triumphs. However, the greatest reward is not found in *coming out of* your trial. Instead it is found in *coming in to* an understanding of self. I met myself in a time of crisis. Sometimes, only crisis can reveal who we are at heart and what we truly believe. Just as we spend time developing our other relationships, our future demands that we get to know ourselves. Self-improvement doesn't come easy. It will take time, some tears and commitment. But if we apply what we know, while diligently searching for what we know we're missing, and then trust God...the process will work for our good!

### The Process

Knowledge that I have to change,
And knowing this change will come,
Is the glue that keeps my mind
As my emotions come undone.

Better than my yesterday,
Because now at least I see.
But frustrations seem to overwhelm
As I stretch to become the real me.

I know that I will overcome
Though right now victory seems far.
But it's hard to see the greater things
When pain comes from the way things are.

Storms rage within my mind,
As I struggle to find my peace.
And though faith whispers, "Change will come."
Time attacks my belief.

I must believe that with each new day
Comes the hope of something new.
And though yesterday and today seem the same,
I'm one day closer to my breakthrough.

To despair is easy,
To hope is the real test.
To stay the same is tempting,
But "the process" is the best!

The process is the step between
Who I am and want to be.
It is wanting more, but having less
It's about trusting what I can't see.

It's the pain of reality,
Mixed with the promise of faith.
It's wanting to move ahead —
But life tells me to wait.
The process is the fire
That produces and causes growth.
It's about wanting to run and wanting to stand,
But knowing that I can't do both!

I know this trial will pass,
But it has been here for a while.
And every time I think it's through,
I realize there's another mile.

To despair would be so easy,
Because I am tired and desire rest.
But I will only become who I really am,
Under the fire of "the process."

> "YOUR GRASS CAN BE GREENER
> — IF YOU WATER IT!"

CHAPTER 5
COMPARISON SHOPPING

The need to say, "Mine is better than," or at the very least, "just as good as yours," almost seems part of human nature. We see it all the time. Little kids play with their toys bragging like future advertising executives about the superiority of their product. "Well, mine can do this, can yours?" they ask, and though they don't come right out and say it, the other kid gets the picture: "Yours is better."

All of our lives we are faced with the temptation to compare ourselves with others and prove that we measure up. In the moments when we've taken a break from engaging in this futile exercise, someone else takes over. Unwitting parents use comparison as a disciplining technique to prod their children to behave, thinking perhaps that if they tell one child how "great" another sibling is at something, that it will produce a miraculous turnaround. Instead, what it usually does is breed contempt between the siblings and inevitably sends out the message, "You're just not good enough — so change!"

A few weeks ago, as I traveled into Manhattan with my

brother, I noticed a woman wearing a beautiful diamond engagement ring. I pointed it out to him and he commented that it wasn't any different from his wife's. In that moment it struck me how subtly comparison can work its way into our everyday perceptions and appreciation of things. I replied, "I didn't say anything about how it compares." It dawned on me that he could not fully appreciate the beauty of the woman's ring because he viewed it in the light of something else.

For some reason that interaction stayed with me all day, and I found myself thinking about the role comparison had played in my own life. For seven years I battled depression, and though there were many factors that contributed to it, comparison played a major role in my negative thinking patterns. Throughout that time my emotions were often screaming about the unfairness of life towards me. I was always looking at the greener grass on the other side. Meanwhile my grass was dying because I spent all my time peeking over the fence.

If you're wasting your time being angry because your best friend can eat a pint of ice cream and not gain weight, forget about it. The hand you have is the one you've been dealt, and how you play the hand is all that matters. You've got to beat comparison by knowing its trump card.

1. **Comparison is a dangerous sport to engage the mind in!** Comparing yourself to someone, and then concluding that you are better can foster arrogance. Arrogance blinds you to the rich lessons found in someone else's experience. We can all learn from each other and can't afford to carelessly discount the input or value of those around us.

2. **Comparison can hide life's blessings!** Arriving at the conclusion that what you have is less could cause you to bypass the power of your gifts and talents. The goal in life

is not to be the "best" anything but you! Know your strengths and your weaknesses, but beyond knowing them, use them. Use your strengths to help others, and where you are weak, surround yourself with people who can help you grow and develop in that area. Commit yourself to personal transformation and watch the doors open to a rich and rewarding life.

3. **Comparison reduces productivity.** The demand to outperform someone else is depleting to the spirit, soul and body. Focus on your finish line. Looking at others will only slow you down. There is a divine task that you are appointed to perform. **Your very existence is God's response to a need in the universe!** You have your own special assignment; don't waste time desiring someone else's.

Our satisfaction with life cannot be based on being "better" than someone else, because inevitably someone will always be smarter, prettier, funnier, etc.... There is room and a need for us all. We are not in a competition. Don't be distracted by comparison's agenda. The only thing you need to be concerned about is getting to know yourself!

### I Know

I told the Lord I was tired
And He whispered, "I Know."
I told Him my eyes were weak and feeble.
I didn't know which way to go.

I told Him I had been crying.
My nights were filled with pain.
I told Him all seemed at a loss and
Nothing had I gained.

I told Him I had lost patience
And that He was moving too slow.
I told Him I needed a breakthrough
And He whispered, "I Know."

I told Him others were prospering,
And living out their dreams.
While I was walking in barrenness
With no hope at all it seemed.

I told the Lord I felt helpless
And I couldn't stand another blow.
But although my storm was raging,
He only whispered, "I Know."

"I Know your hurts and sorrows
I Know what you've been through.
But I Know the power of My word
And the joy I have set before you.

I Know my omniscient power.
I Know that I am in control.
I Know I have redeemed you.
You are delivered, free and whole.

I Know where your focus is
And you have not set it on Me.
I am the God of all creation,
I am He who caused all things to be.

I Know where I am taking you,
The purpose for which you were made.
So set your sights upon Me
And walk the paths that I have laid.

I Know your every feeling.
I've tasted the pain in each tear you've shed.
But I delivered you from your darkness
When I triumphed over death.

Every second on the cross
I lived what you're going through.
But because I've tasted the bitterness,
Life's walk can be sweet for you."

His voice calmed my emotional winds.
He spoke peace into my storm.
He showed me who I really am,
The covenant I'm standing on.

I'm already a victor.
More than a conqueror through Him.
Because of His precious blood,
I know now that I win.

My darkness turned to light.
And although things were still moving slow.
He whispered, "It is finished!"
And I told Him, "Lord,...I Know."

> "FIND THE MEANING OF YOUR
> STRUGGLE, AND YOU FIND THE MEANS
> TO END YOUR STRUGGLE."

CHAPTER 6
WALK ON IT!

It is difficult to HEAL when you have to continually revisit the crime scene or see the "perpetrator" repeatedly. Every time you see them or go there it is like the pain is fresh once more. I struggled with this exact same issue in a community service organization I was once active in.

It was a year and a half into my H.E.A.L.I.N.G.™ process from depression and I had mustered up the courage to participate in life again. I became active in the organization and was soon asked to lend my gifts and passions to various projects. I was blossoming and finding hope again. Things were going smoothly and then, boom, I found myself in the midst of a crisis. To others it may not have been a crisis, but for me — someone who had allowed herself to fade into the background, it was just life telling me once again, "See, getting involved hurts."

I have since gotten over the details of the offense, but I must be honest and tell you that it shook me to my core. I was supposed to be part of a place that brought healing, yet instead I was being hurt. It is hard to understand when you get hurt where you should heal. That is why offenses within the family and church are some of the hardest to overcome. My tender emotions went into a tailspin once more. Everything I had shied away from seemed to be chasing me down. I was hearing rumors about myself that I knew to be false. People suddenly stopped speaking to me, and worst of all, I didn't have any real explanation as to why things had changed.

I struggled for months with the emotions that I had to face. I questioned whether or not I had done something wrong, and then I felt anger and betrayal. My emotions kept going in a never-ending cycle. Some might say, "Well, why not just leave?" Well, I didn't leave because I didn't believe that it was time to leave. Like Kenny Rogers says, "You've got to know when to hold them and know when to fold them." It wasn't my time to fold.

## THE RULES OF THE GAME

One evening I attended a basketball game sponsored by this same organization, at a neighborhood high school gym. As I walked into the gymnasium, many of the people that had started giving me the cold shoulder were there. I wondered to myself, "Lord, how can I keep doing this?" I sat on the bleachers next to a good friend of mine as the game started. During the second quarter, a player injured his ankle and was forced to leave the court. The referee called for a time out and a new player came in to replace him. Just as suddenly as it had stopped, the game began again.

Meanwhile, the injured player sat on the sidelines grabbing his ankle. His face contorted in pain and changed various hues of red. I was sure that he was about to burst into tears.

One of his teammates tightened his shoelaces in an effort to stabilize the ankle and evenly distribute the pressure.

Suddenly, the player stood and began limping around the court. I watched in shock. From the look of his fall, I was sure that he was going to be carried out on a stretcher. I turned to my friend and asked, "What is he doing? Is he crazy?" And to this she responded, "He's got to walk on it."

In that moment I learned an important lesson. Pain and other emotional wounds have to be walked on. I couldn't surrender my joy and emotions to people who didn't understand me, and neither can you. You cannot afford to give in to the things that desire to cripple you. If you don't exercise your "right to happiness," you will atrophy in your state of pain. You must keep moving!

When life offers you unexpected valleys, make up in your mind that you are going to get through them. You cannot control how others choose to respond to you or what happens to you, but you are the only one who controls what happens in you. Don't allow hurts and rejections to cap your potential.

Pain will eventually subside as you regain control of your thinking patterns and emotions. Once you have everything in the proper perspective, it will make things more manageable. I thought the player was more seriously injured than he really was. Yes, he was in pain but he did what needed to be done — and then kept on going! There comes a point when you have to stop nurturing your pain and instead nourish your right to live. Many of us are trapped in emotional time warps. We were hurt in the game of life, but we never got up from the place we were injured and the game continued without us.

Life is like that basketball game that only stopped for a few seconds to allow the player to leave. Once he was off the court, someone else was called in and the game resumed. People will only stop for a moment to allow you a "time out," but afterwards it will be business as usual for everyone else. It is up to you whether or not you finish out the game. Get off the bench and get back in the game, because this world needs you!

## Never Lose Your Stuff

I know it gets hard
And the way gets rough,
But never let your trials
Take your stuff.

Though others stand around
And count you out,
Never place your faith
In their fears and doubts.

It looks like you've lost,
But it's just a bluff.
Stand your ground
And fight for your stuff.

Been hit in the place
Where it hurts most of all.
The blow was so hard
You can't walk, so you crawl.

Problems to your left
Disappointments to your right.
You're just getting whipped
It's not even a fight.

You're getting too weak
It's getting too tough,
But you still got the goods
If you've still got your stuff.

Don't let it crush you,
Or cause a break in your stride.
Your enemies don't want your things,
They want the hope you have inside.

So push with all you've got
Even cry if you must.
But look your problems in the eye
And say, "You can't take my stuff."

Your stuff is you
It's what makes you unique,
It's what causes you to shine
When all else looks bleak.

It's your smile,
Your walk,
Your style,
Your strut.
It's all that you are
Don't ever give it up!

God put it in you,
And though others want to shake it.
They didn't make you
So they have no right to take it.

Let the storm clouds rise
Let the seas get rough
But don't you never, ever
Ever, never
To whosoever
Over whatsoever
Just stand forever
Endure the hard weather
But never lose your stuff!

*H:* Help While You're Hurting

*E:* Enjoy Life's Process

*A:* **Accept and Anticipate Change**

*L:* Let Go…

*I:* Itemize Your Issues and Images

*N:* Navigate Your Needs

*G:* Grow with Gratitude

# STRATEGY THREE

*Accept and Anticipate Change*

Change can be very frightening when it is beyond your control. But change is inevitable. If we are going to be successful and live balanced lives, we must learn to accept and cooperate with the changing seasons we encounter in our emotions, careers and relationships. Most of our struggles with change are rooted in improper identification with external factors and influences. We allow ourselves to be defined by things outside of us. But it is what lives inside of us that makes us who we are. You can survive and thrive in any change of circumstance when you have confidence in yourself. Though change can be challenging, it should not be feared or dreaded. It is staying the same that should alarm us. Change should be anticipated because every moment of life is pregnant with opportunity. Occasionally, opportunity comes disguised as adversity, but with faith and patience we can work our way through to the miracle.

"DON'T FEAR CHANGE,
FEAR STAGNATION!"

CHAPTER 7
GROWING PAINS

We are creatures of habit and comfort, gravitating towards what feels good and comes easiest. We desire security and comfort and fear anything that threatens to disturb them. We fear the unknown and often approach it with negativity rather than expectation and anticipation. The future can be faced confidently when we recognize God's love for us. Understanding this love assures us that regardless of what we may face, we are equipped for the challenge. Failure is not to be feared, for it is merely a necessary ingredient in our future success and the maturation of our character.

One of the most painful feelings in life is feeling as though we have been "left behind." We deal with it all of our lives. In first grade, we find out that our best friend has been put in a different class and we feel abandoned. But it gets harder as we go along. After high school, decisions for college must be made. Then comes the really hard part — people move away, find love, get married and then start families. When it happens for others and not for you — it can make change an unwelcome visitor in your world.

## SEPARATION ANXIETY

I remember a particularly painful time of transition in my own life. I have a sister-friend who is the Willona to my Florida, and the Ethel to my Lucy. Throughout our high school and college years, we were inseparable. If you saw one, the other was not too far behind. After graduation, she had the nerve to meet and fall in love with a wonderful man. Having survived past relationships and dates, I initially thought that this one would dissipate. Like a virus, I thought it just needed to run its course and be worked out of her system. Imagine my alarm when I realized that he was here to stay! I was so afraid of this change that I fought it with everything I could. I was not ready for things to be different.

For years I always knew what I would be doing on the weekends. We would hang out, catch an old movie and order Chinese food. I never really worried about being alone because I knew that she would be there. Then suddenly, she had a life of her own and everything didn't involve me. I would love to tell you that I handled the transition with grace and maturity — but that would be a lie. I will be honest and tell you that I cut the fool! I cried, I plotted, I complained, and when that didn't work I became cold and distant towards her boyfriend. I ignored him when he came to visit her, and I confess that there were times when I would conveniently forget to tell her he called. My shenanigans only served to strain our relationship and put distance between us. I couldn't accept the fact that she was entering into a new phase of life without me. I felt left behind.

I will never forget the day that I realized I had to accept change. She'd received tickets to a screening of a movie that we both wanted to see. It never crossed my mind that she wouldn't invite me to come along. She knew how much I wanted to see this film. One small problem — he wanted to see it too. Though she tried to explain that his desire meant something different, not necessarily more than my going — I couldn't understand it. I just remember feeling angry and betrayed when she didn't invite me. In retrospect, I realize that it wasn't a "right or wrong" decision, but it was the choice she had to make.

## FROM CHANGE TO CHANGED

I knew then that things had changed. We were no longer in a process. The transition was completed, and I had a choice to make. I would either accept him as a part of her life or I would lose the friendship all together.

The transition was not easy and there were times I thought our friendship wouldn't survive. I had become so dependent on the relationship that I had neglected to develop myself in some important areas. Sure, I always knew that she would meet someone and get married. I knew that I eventually would meet a good man and get married as well. But in my mind, the timing of it would all be convenient for me. I had always figured it would happen at the same time for both of us. I never imagined that I would be left behind.

From that experience, I have learned many things that continue to stimulate my personal development. "He" has now become one of my closest friends; in fact he is the best male friend that I have. His experience, wisdom and thirst for knowledge have been a source of inspiration and encouragement to me. But if I had continued to fight the change I would have lost my best friend and I would never be enjoying the relationship that he and I share.

More importantly, the changes forced me to stretch. I learned that I must never lose sight of my individuality, regardless of how much I enjoy the comfort of a relationship.

I must always challenge myself to develop new friendships and be respectful and appreciative of those who are in my life. I learned that my value, happiness and peace cannot come from my relationships with other human beings. It has to come from my relationship with God.

Sometimes we find ourselves in a comfortable place, and though it feels good, it doesn't always demand much growth on our part. Emotional muscle needs to be exercised and it is a good thing when we are stretched out of our comfort zone and forced to make new discoveries about ourselves. Fear-filled messages want to intimidate and paralyze you. They want to push you into a small corner and keep you from participating in life. But don't run from the changes life wants to bring you. I know it can be outright terrifying, but the lessons of self-discovery that lie ahead are priceless! It's all designed to work for your good and in the end it will be better than you could ever imagine.

## Change

Sometimes like a breeze,
Carrying sweet fragrance in its hand.
So does change come gently to me.

Sometimes like a hurricane,
With destruction in its winds
Sometimes change rips through me.

Bringing me joy, sweet relief and some pain.
Bringing me sorrow, some sunshine and rain.
These are the ways change comes to me.

Accustomed to my routine,
To the life I've defined.
Growing stiff in my comforts,
Sometimes stunted in my mind.

Forever challenging the way I believe.
Forever pushing me to grow and achieve.
Will I bend?
Will I break?
Will I stand up?
Or will I fall?
Will I throw in the towel?
Or will I fight for it all?

Stretching and shaking me,
Making me reach.
Discovering inner strength —
These are the lessons change can teach.

A powerful force,
A constant in life.
A bond between mankind,
Sometimes darkness, sometimes light.

Setting in order,
Removing to rearrange.
A sure companion in life
Is the force called change.

"MEMORIES REHEARSED
CAN BE MORE POWERFUL THAN
YOUR PRESENT REALITY."

CHAPTER 8
LIVE OR MEMOREX?

I once watched the movie *Sunset Boulevard*, starring Gloria Swanson and William Holden for a film course in college. The movie is about a former Hollywood starlet who has aged and faded into anonymity but refuses to accept the fact that her time has passed. Consequently, she lives in a world devoid of reality and shaped solely by her imagination.

While most of us are not this far removed from the reality of our lives, I believe we often avoid facing the harsh truths about ourselves. Like the movie, we live out of our imagination. We interact with others based on what we perceive, but often our perceptions are based on past experiences and relationships.

Though the truth can be a hard pill to swallow, the only way we will experience real emotional and spiritual freedom is by acknowledging the truth and facing it. The truth we know makes us free. Be honest about your reality! Denying the existence of certain things will not make them go away, it will only serve to put your mental, emotional and spiritual health in jeopardy.

## BURY IT

Dead things develop a stench and leave a foul odor that every-
one recognizes as death. But people who have become accus-
tomed to the scent never seem to be bothered by it. Grudges
and bitterness stink, and the odor is expressed in our atti-
tudes. As difficult as it may be, we must learn to accept some
things without question.

My father passed away on New Year's Day, 1999. I spoke to
him that very morning and we said our "I love yous" and our
"good-byes." About twelve hours later, he was gone. I enjoyed
a rich relationship with my father and his death devastated
me. Like all relationships, we had our issues, but I was his
"baby girl" and his "left sock." In the days before he died we
discussed all kinds of things, like what we would dance to at my
wedding — even though I wasn't in love or about to get mar-
ried. We just took it for granted that he would be around for
that wonderful day in my life.

There have been times when I've cried in anger as I've faced
problems that I would normally turn to him to discuss. I miss
him so much when I need to know if I'm paying the right
amount for the mechanic to fix my car. I miss him when I hear
"You Send Me" by Sam Cooke — that's the song we were sup-
posed to dance to. I miss him every day of my life. Many peo-
ple think they know why my father died when he was just 52.

My first response to my father's death was to question why
God allowed it to happen. It seemed unfair that he was sud-
denly ripped from my family's life and where his strength
once comforted us, there was now only pain and emptiness.
For a moment, I struggled to wrap my mind around it. But
how do you cope with life's mysteries when they seem so
unfair? I quickly realized the futility of these thoughts and
refused to invest more emotional energy into trying to
understand why. Honestly, there was no answer that would

ease my pain. For my own peace of mind, I had to first accept the fact that he was gone. Once I released the need to comprehend his death, I was able to move forward with joy and anticipation for my future. Then, instead of being stuck on the loss, I could focus on the gift that he was, and continues to be, in my life. In accepting and, to a degree, embracing my father's death, the door has opened for father figures. Though no one can ever take his place, there are those who are always there for me and help me with challenges — from installing the air conditioner to knowing the best qualities to look for in a potential mate.

We have been taught that in order to solve a problem, we must first understand it. In most cases, that is true. But there are cases that defy the odds and our only response to them is faith and acceptance. We must learn to grow comfortable with the fact that sometimes understanding doesn't come until we accept. Sometimes understanding comes years down the road. Sometimes understanding doesn't come at all, and we must learn to be comfortable with that too.

## Dead Things

Dead things have a way of living
In the corners of your mind.
They eat at the resolutions
And peace you seek to find.

Issues you thought were over
Come to haunt you with defeat.
And though your spirit would like a change,
Your flesh is decidedly weak.

Feelings of pain resurface
With a force that makes them new.
A web of negative memories
Reach out to entangle you.

Paralyzed with discouragement
Crippled by the power of fear.
Your heart grows weak from unfulfilled hopes,
As your vision is blurred by tears.

Dead things have a way of living,
Even when they look healed.
They grow and fester
Stink and rot
And destroy all that you try to build.

Dead things have a way of traveling
Through the measurement called time.
The bitter taste of tainted mother's milk
Can cross generation's lines.

We bury the bodies of loved ones
Whose spirits have been set free.
And just as we leave them beneath the earth.
We must also let dead things be.

> "HOPE — THE FOUNDATION
> FOR SUCCESSFUL LIVING!"

CHAPTER 9
## WINNER OR WHINER?

### WEIGHED IN THE BALANCE

Our subconscious and conscious minds are engaged in a never-ending dialogue. We become so accustomed to their conversations that we learn to tune them out at an early age. Without our approval, they have formed an alliance that governs our lives — our personalities, characters, and experiences.

We have messages coming at us every moment of the day. Some are blatant, and others are subtle. Nevertheless, they all have an effect. Any woman who watches television can tell you that commercials with buxom women running along the beach automatically make them analyze their own bodies' shortcomings. They've gotten the message: This is what beauty looks like, if you don't look like beauty — guess what? You're not beautiful! No one has to say it, but you get the picture. If you fail to confront that thought it will stay with you and, before you know it, you'll hear it again when you're at the mall and an attractive guy passes by. Surely, he wouldn't be interested in you — you don't have the look most guys want. We deal with these messages every day of our lives and they impact the way we relate to others and ourselves.

Somewhere along the line, due to disappointments and failure, you may have internalized the message "Nothing ever works out for me. Things just always seem to go wrong. I just can't catch a break." It may have become your philosophy about life that whenever opportunity comes looking for someone, it bypasses you. Not because of who you are, but because you can't recognize opportunity. You have chosen to acquaint yourself with failure.

## BETTER THAN MAYBELLINE

Two individuals can have very similar experiences that can crush one, yet inspire the other to dig deeper and to pursue more achievements. The difference between the two people is their attitude. One expects failure and the other anticipates possibility. I believe that positive anticipation is the most important grooming product in any woman or man's beauty regimen. Anticipation beautifies you and attracts opportunity. We are all drawn to people who carry their own sunshine and those who aren't are usually intimidated by it. It stands to reason that if you attract more people, you attract more opportunity. Opportunity is out there looking for someone to hook up with, and it always gravitates toward anticipation.

I know that it can be hard to anticipate and have hope when things have disappointed you repeatedly. Investing in hope can sometimes be too painful and hopelessness can provide a false security. Negative people always get what they expect. But you are cheating yourself of possibility. Never let an experience become your god by determining what you can and cannot expect out of life. Never surrender your life to the things that have gone wrong. Being bitter and hopeless is draining to the emotions and stressful to the body. From a mental, physical and pure common sense standpoint it is better to be hopeful and disappointed than to walk around hopeless and accepting of negative results. Sometimes events that took a moment can live a lifetime because we allow them to permanently disfigure our expectations from life. In healing from depression, I realized that I had to dare to believe again. Hopelessness was stealing days out of my life. I have since learned that like everything else around us our emotions experience four seasons. The key is learning to adapt to the season you are in, while preparing for the next one. We will all experience winter when nothing seems to grow. But your roots can grow deep during this cold season. Emotional winter is the time to focus on becoming more responsible. It is a time to evaluate and make the necessary attitude changes in your life so that you will be ready for spring. Even in the Antarctic, spring will come after winter. It is inevitable and the natural course of all life. Hard times are only temporary. They have a predetermined beginning and an end. In spring, new opportunities will come. In summer, things will continue to be nourished and grow, but you must protect what you have sown. In fall, reap the results of your efforts. And, yes, winter will come again. Be prepared to endure.

## PATTI SAID IT RIGHT!

An attitude change is in order. Anticipate! Start with some small objective, and watch as things begin to change. You will walk taller with more confidence. You'll feel better because you're not walking around in a defensive position but, instead, you are secure in the goodness of life.

Learn from the past, but keep the past in its place — behind you. Enjoy the present and hope for the future. A new day can

begin at any moment. All it requires is a shift in your think-
ing, a change in your mind — a transition in your perspective.
I don't care how today started for you; it can end on a differ-
ent note. You can have a new day. So, go ahead. What are you
waiting for?

### New Day

New Day,
Different way.
Same games,
Can't play.
No time to stay
I've got to make a change!

Small talk, chit chat.
Hands out, now I lack.
We've already tried that,
I've got to make a change!

Played with you, got fleas.
Your "needs," almost killed me.
I once was blind, but now I see.
I've got to make a change!

Day and night, I've cried.
Can't win, why try?
Don't believe that lie,
I've got to make a change!

Boo hoo, why me?
I've got two, but she's got three.
Grow up and be free!
I've got to make a change!

Skies black, emotions blue.
Self-pity I am through with you.
Got too much, I'm going to
I've got to make a change!

Times are bad
God is good.
This will end as it should.
Have I done all I could?
Nope...
Because I've got to make a change!

*H:* Help While You're Hurting

*E:* Enjoy Life's Process

*A:* Accept and Anticipate Change

*L:* **Let Go...**

*I:* Itemize Your Issues and Images

*N:* Navigate Your Needs

*G:* Grow with Gratitude

# STRATEGY FOUR

## Let Go...

You're not losing; you're just making room. We all know what it is like to stay where we realize we've already been too long. We know what it is to hold on to a relationship because we fear being alone. Life is a series of steps and you can't fully move on to the next without leaving the one before. There is a comfort in the familiar that keeps us holding on long after one season has passed. It is crucial to remember that you can't have what you really want until you are ready to move out of your comfort zone. Challenge yourself by releasing negative thought patterns that stunt you, negative people that limit you, and negative situations that poison you. Weaning won't work for some of your issues — you're going to have to quit cold turkey.

"THE PROBLEM ISN'T WHAT YOU'VE BEEN
GETTING. IT'S WHAT YOU'VE KEPT!"

CHAPTER 10
BAD INVESTMENTS

## EMOTIONAL SAVINGS ACCOUNT

"Keep quiet."

"Keep still."

"Keep it to yourself!"

"Keep out."

"Keep shut."

"Keep it down."

Rage is the result of keeping too much. We were not designed to continually suppress negative emotions — it is destructive to the spirit. This principle is best demonstrated in the body, which is designed to daily release toxins and infections through sweat and other channels. Imagine the damage that would be done to our bodies if everything we ingested remained stored. We wouldn't survive because the poisons would kill us. Likewise, emotional suppression has the same affect on the spirit.

If you lack the courage to stand up for yourself and develop open communication in your relationships, you are going to find yourself physically sick and stressed out. Ulcers, headaches and indigestion are just some of the ways that pent-up emotions express themselves. When we suppress our feelings, we end up abused and victimized. Eventually that pain will channel itself into anger, because even victims get angry. In fact, they get angrier than most people do. The anger at feeling helpless and abused develops and festers into rage.

A characteristic of rage is that it rarely releases it arsenal on those who inflict the pain and commit the trespass. Rage is usually reserved for innocent bystanders and possibly even loved ones who represent no real threat to us. Our employers make us angry, and instead of dealing with them in a professional, yet firm manner, we swallow the mistreatment. A co-worker takes credit for a project you completed, and rather than confronting him/her, you harbor resentment in your heart. These resentments are stored and then erupt to the surface when your spouse forgets to pick up the dry cleaning. Now they're the "most selfish, inconsiderate and irresponsible so and so, who never takes your feelings into account!"

## CLOSE THE ACCOUNT!

Stop keeping everything you are given, because some of it is not yours. It is time for you to throw it away. You barely have room for all the good, because your life is too cluttered with the things you should have discarded long ago. You're cranky and irritable, and it seems like you've got one last nerve that everybody keeps jumping on!

Here's a bit of insight...Clean off your plate and realize that your problem isn't in what you've been getting. The problem is what you've kept!

## 2 Faces of Rage

**HIS SIDE:**

I walk into the store,
And your eyes follow me.
I've only been here a minute,
But you've decided what I will be.

To you I am a criminal,
Come to steal what you've worked for.
But, a moment ago I was a lawyer,
Until I walked into your door.

You don't even know me,
Where I'm from or who I am.
You don't know where I've been in life,
But in your eyes I've been damned.

My skin is not white,
It's a God given natural tan.
And the black cloud rising within me,
Is the rage of a young black man.

Rage against a system,
That seeks to define my every move.
Rage at an absentee father,
Who felt manhood had to be proved.

Rage against your ignorance,
That seeks to put me in a cage.
Insecurity in my true self,
That masks itself as rage.

Each day this rage is growing,
But I won't seek help from up above.
And because I refuse to control it,
I'll turn it on those I love.


## HER SIDE:

Oh, I know you really love me baby.
I know you're sorry you made me cry.
I know that we can work it out,
If we give it one more try.

I know you only hit me,
Because of the things I said.
And though my body is black and blue,
I still want you in my bed.

You were the first one to "love" me,
And make me feel complete.
And if you tried to walk out that door,
I'd lie down at your feet.

But sometimes when you hold me,
I feel like we're on a different page.
And even though I can't let you go...
My heart still fills with rage.

Rage because with every kiss,
Gentle words are betrayed by fists.
Rage because I don't love myself,
So I take abuse from someone else.

Rage against your father,
Who never taught you to be a man.
And rage against my Daddy,
Who didn't love me as I am.

Rage because though I've suffered,
At the hands of someone else.
The real poison that is rotting inside,
Is my rage against myself.

"FAITH ISN'T ALWAYS STANDING.
SOMETIMES IT'S A FREE-FALL."

CHAPTER 11
INTERNAL RENOVATIONS

## DRESS FOR THE SEASON

There is a difference between losing and letting go. Understanding the difference between them can be a hard lesson to learn. The distinction is subtle but significant. Losing means giving up something that you should have fought to keep. Letting go means you want to keep it and you have to fight to give it up.

As the times and seasons of our lives change, we must be willing to change with them. Wearing a swimsuit in the dead of winter is not just inappropriate, it is also dangerous. Similarly, our patterns of behavior must change as we enter into new phases of life. There are some people you used to feel comfortable with, but can't hang out with anymore. There are some places you used to go, but can no longer visit. Life changes and you must adjust to its flow. Sometimes, it's not even a matter of letting go because things or people are hurting you — it's letting go because they're not improving you. Letting go can be even harder than holding on. The release of the known in order to embrace the unknown requires tremendous courage.


## TEMPER TANTRUMS

On a recent trip to Wal-Mart with my three-year-old nephew, we visited the children's book section. Books of every size and kind lined the shelves. As I picked up the different titles to review them, each and every selection sent him into tantrum mode. At the top of his lungs he whined, "Mine, mine!" I grew increasingly embarrassed as other customers looked at me accusingly as if I had done something wrong to him. Not one for public scenes, I gave up my authority as the adult in the situation and gave him the books. Without fail, whatever I picked up sent him into another round of screaming out "Mine!" In a matter of moments, his little arms were filled to capacity.

As we were standing there my eyes came across one of my favorite childhood toys, the Viewmaster! Remembering the countless hours of joy it brought me, my hands reached towards it. Before I could even touch it he began to whine. His arms were completely full but his eyes wanted more. The only solution to avoid another scene was to leave the Viewmaster on the shelf. I couldn't help but think how he would have enjoyed the Viewmaster if he hadn't been so obsessed with having to have everything in his hands. Naturally my mind started contemplating the many times I may have shut myself off from a blessing, simply because I refused to let go of what I was holding in my hand. How many times has refusing to let go of my opinion of a person caused me to miss out on who they really are and on a possibly great relationship?

## GET IN THE PASSING LANE

Most of us agree that there are things we need to let go of. We know we've been trying to get water from the proverbial rock and it's time to move on to a new camping site. Letting go can be difficult. But you never know what you are missing out on, until you let go. I was once talking with a friend who was contemplating breaking up with her boyfriend. She kept expressing how nice he was and how she didn't want to hurt his feelings. Then she'd go on to say that he just wasn't what she was really looking for in her life. And then she'd bounce back again to how she didn't want to hurt him. Frustrated with her indecisiveness, I used the following analogy to help her see that she wasn't doing him any favors by staying.

Have you ever been in a store and saw an item that you knew you wanted? But someone was standing in front of you looking at it trying to make a decision. You peek around them and see that it is the last one of its kind, so you stand there in silent impatience and wait for them to make up their mind. They flip it over and view it from different angles. Meanwhile, it is exactly what you've been looking for. If they would just get out of the way, you would take it. Sometimes, your refusal to let go is blocking someone else's blessings. Your dead end job is somebody's dream job, but they can't get to it because you are in the way. What's more is that sometimes people are standing in your way with their indecisiveness.

## SPRING CLEANING

As you read these words, various people, situations and things are coming to your mind. In fact, when you read the chapter title it caught your attention. You know what you need to let go of — it's time to clean house. Time to rummage through the closets of your mind and the storage bins of your heart. Time to pack up some things and throw them away. Sentimental attachments must go as well, because they are creating too much clutter in your life. As you clean and sort through issues, just remind yourself that you're not losing — you're only making room!

## Let Go

Let Go,
Even though you want to hold on
To the memory of what used to be.
In releasing the past, you'll find new hope
And the strength you need to be free.

Though beautiful the past may be,
Embrace what the future brings.
Yesterday was only a glimpse
Of tomorrow's greater things.

Let Go,
Even though all that's inside
Wants to hold on to what you know.
Life has lessons that need to be learned,
But sometimes you must let go.

Though thoughts of change
Evoke inside feelings of despair and doom.
When you let go of times gone by,
You're not losing; you're just making room.

Room for the wrongs to be made right
And for greatness to be made.
Let go of the things that are in your sight,
So you can have the things you've prayed.

"You're overcome and overwhelmed,"
Says the voice of hopeless defeat.
But it all depends on where you stand —
Sometimes your victory is in your retreat.

The things you're holding do not make you,
Though at times you feel they do.
People's eyes may hold a reflection —
But that doesn't mean it's you.

Life holds many uncertainties
And it will deal you many stormy blows.
But, sometimes safety is not in the anchor —
It is found in letting go.

Ride out the storm you're facing,
Embrace it so that you can grow.
And remember, faith doesn't always stand —
Sometimes faith lets go!

> "KNOW YOUR VALUE,
> OR YOU'LL ALWAYS BE UNDERSOLD."

CHAPTER 12
GET THE LOAF!

## ARE YOU IN THE BARGAIN BIN?

You can't walk into a department store and pick out a hundred-dollar dress and tell the sales person, "I know this dress is a hundred dollars, but I don't think it is worth that much. I am going to give you fifty dollars instead." You will soon realize your mistake as the security guard escorts you out the door. Either you pay the price, or you do without the merchandise. The same must be true of our interpersonal transactions. In your relationships you must set the parameters as to how others will deal with you. If you don't know what you want out of life, you will settle for whatever comes your way.

We feed people the information they use in their interactions with us. By confidently walking into a room with a smile and greeting everyone, you have made a statement about how you expect to be treated. You've told them that you know who you are. Walk into the same room with your eyes on the floor and offer up a "limp-wristed" handshake and you have told them that you are to be dismissed.

If you don't know your worth, you will settle for whatever asking price is offered. Millions of women are involved in extramarital affairs for years at a time because it's meeting a need in their lives. They know that the husband is not going to risk his wife and children for their relationship. They know it! Yet these same women will cut themselves off from the attentions of available men, despite their deep desire to be married and have a family of their own.

## HIGH CALORIE SNACKS!

I've got news for you. If you really want to get married and have a family, don't settle for the temporary satisfaction of an extramarital affair. You only feel good while he's there; once he's gone you'll feel empty all over again. It is beneath you to be with someone who can't be publicly identified with you. You convince yourself it is love, but what you are really getting are crumbs. The spouse gets the commitment and security, while you get to nurse a broken heart because deep down inside you know that it will never be more than a "part-time, if I can find the time" deal! A crumb is a leftover — it is what remains when the best is gone. A crumb is a crumb whether it falls to the ground or is served on a silver platter. Don't be fooled by its presentation. Call it what it is. No matter how big the crumbs are they don't provide the nourishment and satisfaction of a healthy, balanced meal. You will starve to death trying to live off the crumbs that others wish to feed you. Until you get "sick and tired" and decide to demand satisfaction from life, you are destined to eat others' crumbs, getting love and respect only when they feel you deserve it.

## FLIP THE COIN

By the same token, make sure that you're not the person distributing the crumbs. Make sure that you are giving your relationships your all. You have a right to respect and fulfillment, but you have the responsibility of first being and doing what you desire most. Balance is knowing what you deserve, while fulfilling your responsibilities to others. You must know what you are required to be, to give and to do in your relationships.

Before complaining about the way people treat you, check the messages you've been sending out. Have you conveyed to others your need for healthy love, respect and affection? Or have you told them that their crumbs are good enough for you?

### No More Crumbs!

Either give me all,
Or give me none.
But I'm not taking
Anymore of your crumbs.

No more little bit of this,
And a little bit of that.
No more eating up the meat,
While giving me bone and fat.

All my life I've eaten
What was left behind.
Others eating melon,
My mouth cut up by the rind.

I may not be a genius,
And at times I've been outright dumb.
But I've got enough sense to know
That I'm better than your crumbs.

You've been giving less,
And I've been wanting more.
And since the two can't seem to meet,
I'm walking out the door.

I don't expect perfection,
But I do expect a friend.
I don't know where it started,
But I do know where it ends.

Subtraction and division seem
To be this relationship's sum.
But here's a bit of addition,
I'm giving you back all your crumbs.

You've got all the money,
And you've got all the wealth.
But today I finally realized —
I'm better off by myself.

Bake them — they can be croutons,
And bread the best snapper from the sea.
There are a thousand things to do with them,
But not one of them is good enough for me.

I'm not walking away,
I'm about to run...
But, I've truly forgiven you
For all that you've done.

Cause I'm tired out,
I've had enough.
I've given up,
Don't want your stuff.

With God, I know the wounds will heal.
No more talking.  We can't make a deal.
I'm hungry now.  I need a full course meal.

NO MORE CRUMBS!

> ## "CRISIS IS A MATCHMAKER —
> ## IT INTRODUCES YOU TO YOURSELF!"

CHAPTER 13
## THE FIX IS IN

### NO 900 NUMBERS NEEDED!

Do you want to know why you are so afraid of letting go? Do you want to know why your stomach ties in knots when you think of change? I will tell you what I think. I think it is because you have not yet made the connection that life has something better to offer you. You don't believe that your best days are still ahead.

There is nothing that you need to lose sleep over and you don't need to visit a psychic to find the answers you are searching for — the answers lie within you. The key is in your response. God has already provided everything you need to make it. You must learn how to tap into it!

Instead of stopping to assess your value and get in touch with how special and wonderful you are, perhaps you have chosen to find your validation in the opinions that others form about you. If you understood the purpose of your life, you would cease trying to manipulate public opinion and find contentment in who you are. Stop fretting over what you don't have and start using the resources that are already in your hand. Using them will open the door to more.

## BE A GOLD DIGGER!

Defeat cannot operate in your life without your permission. Sure you may fail and things may not always go the way you plan, but defeat isn't an option until you decide to give up completely. In times of great challenge, you must look within for the strength and comfort you need. Believe me when I say that God has given you a treasure chest of ideas just waiting to be discovered. As you focus on these things, you will gain the strength you need to ask for help. Help is not asking someone else to do it for you, help is asking for input and wisdom that will help you find your way. The situation may feel hopeless, but as long as you're still breathing there is still hope!

## LATE-BREAKING NEWS

Do you remember the last time you were down and out? You didn't think you could make it then, but you did. Just when it seemed you were out for the count, you got up and made it to another round! The odds were stacked against you, but you made it. You don't even know how, but one morning you woke up and realized that it was a new day.

Your victory wasn't on the television, and it didn't make the evening news. Ted Koppel didn't request an exclusive interview, but it was the greatest moment of your life! When nobody else could coach you through, the message came from within you!

## It's In Me!

Thought you whipped me.
Thought you stripped me.
Thought you took away my pride.
Thought you beat me.
Thought you'd cheat me.
And like a child I'd run and hide.

Let me school you.
Let me tell you.
Let me end the mystery.
You can't take my convictions,
Because I've got it all in me.

Running tricks,
Running schemes,
Trying to scandalize my name.
Spreading lies like a cancer,
Trying to put my life to shame.

Shaking heads, shaking fingers.
Going by what you see,
Little did you know
That my peace was still in me.

You were talking and stalking,
Threatening to destroy.
Pulling stunts, pulling tricks,
It was all just a ploy.

Told you once, told you twice.
Never go by what you see.
My joy is what you're looking for,
But I've got it all in me.

Depression came to press me
And smother all my dreams.
I was ripped. I almost slipped.
I was torn at the seams.

Discouragement came to taunt me.
To force a last stand.
My demise was all worked out,
But God had another plan.

"She's still standing,"
I heard them marvel.
"Her head is still held high."
They didn't know that in my midnight.
God refused to let me die.

"Rise Up!"
He told me.
"Press On!"
I heard him say.
"Weeping was for the nighttime.
Look Up!
It's a brand new day."

Told you once, told you twice,
Now I'll make it three.
I take a lickin'
And keep on tickin'
Because I've got it all in me.

Again and again,
I've told you.
This one is for free.
You'll never be the winner,
When you fight the God in me.

*H:* Help While You're Hurting

*E:* Enjoy Life's Process

*A:* Accept and Anticipate Change

*L:* Let Go...

*I:* **Itemize Your Issues and Images**

*N:* Navigate Your Needs

*G:* Grow with Gratitude

# STRATEGY FIVE

*Itemize Your Issues and Images*

Everyone in the world has issues! Don't let them fool you. Whether they have a GED or a Ph.D., whether they are single or married, rich or poor. And these issues don't stay isolated in our hearts and minds. They are expressed in our relationships, finances and thoughts. Whatever you are experiencing in your life right now is a result of something in your heart. Refusing to face your issues is emotional suicide. You cannot afford to lie to yourself. You must be your own best friend as you face the issues and images that have confined and defined your existence. Until you find out what everything stems from, you can't get rid of any of it. Free yourself of others' definitions and opinions. Dare to journey to yourself. Some people are more concerned about maintaining their perception of you than dealing with who you really are. You have to know what you want, how you want it and what you're willing to do and become to get it. Your job is to express yourself fully, through and sometimes in spite of it all.

> "YOU CAN'T STOP WHAT PASSES
> THROUGH YOUR MIND, BUT YOU MUST
> CONTROL WHAT STAYS THERE."

CHAPTER 14
SUPERHEROES, AND OTHER
CHILDHOOD MYTHS

## ORIGINS

Where are you from? It's one of the first questions we usually ask someone upon introduction. Yet very rarely do we apply the same question to the origins of the thoughts and emotions we experience daily. Instead we allow a fixed thought system that we have never investigated to govern our lives and relationships. In order for H.E.A.L.I.N.G.™ to begin so we can advance in our lives past the everyday challenges that subtly wear us down, we must identify and clarify the I's of our lives: our issues and our images.

As I said before, some of our attitudes go unchecked and we are unaware of them, until they rear their ugly heads at inappropriate moments. One afternoon as I sat in my car waiting for a friend, I noticed a young couple. As I watched them together, it dawned on me that their intimacy was something I wanted to have in my own life. But at the same time, the idea of being openly affectionate and expressive with my emotions not only frightened me, it actually made me physically ill. Part of me was jealous of the way the young man looked into his companion's eyes as if she were the only woman alive. But another part of me was critical of her willingness to be so transparent with her feelings for him.

## WARRING WITHIN

I was confused by the tension between my thoughts and desires. How could I be so repulsed by something that I wanted? I realized that I wanted it, but was afraid to have it. Not only was I afraid to have it, I was embarrassed by the very fact that I wanted it. I questioned myself as to why I felt this way and inevitably this led me back to the place where most definitions begin for all of us — childhood.

## WONDER WOMAN WENT OFF THE AIR!

As a child, I never saw my mother cry. I mean never, not during a sad movie, not when she hurt herself physically. She would cringe and wince, but tears were never shed. I watched my mother face a parent's worst nightmare — losing a child. In front of her children she continued to stand like a knight in "un-chinked" armor.

I now know that she held back her emotions because she felt it was the way to protect us. She knew that our security and stability was rooted in her. We watched the way she and my father handled situations to gauge how life was going. But as a child I misunderstood her actions. Though she never actually said baring your emotions was a sign of weakness, I interpreted it from her actions. Strength to me meant that you didn't cry. So I suppressed my emotions and grew up holding my problems and insecurities inside.

During the unsettling time of adolescence, I attempted to handle the issues of high school crushes, rejection, childish betrayals and the more serious things alone. I wanted to be strong like my mother and handle it all on my own. I had Wonder Woman syndrome before I was even a woman. I did not know that emotional suppression is a self-inflicted wound.

Like me, many people look to their parents as the model for what "adulthood" should look like. As children, we stand in their shoes and forecast our future based on what we see in them and their experiences. I knew my mother loved me, but her love was not expressed in a way that I could fully understand or appreciate when I was younger. So in many ways I attempted to parent myself on the path to emotional maturity. It is only now as an adult that I realize how I misjudged her and how my failure to communicate with her caused me to suffer needlessly. Arriving at a premature judgment about someone or something cuts short the process of inspection and prevents further evolution in your thinking about the subject. In essence, you close the door on possibility.


## SAY IT, DO IT AND SAY IT AGAIN

As parents we must make sure we teach and live the messages we want our children to learn. Failing to do this can lead them to arrive at the wrong conclusions about life — and us. Quite often it is our parents' flaws and imperfections that we choose to deny the most. We refuse to see their faults because we fear finding the same qualities in ourselves.

It is unfair to hold your parents to superhuman standards. Like you, they are flawed people trying to find their way. Don't feel guilty about facing the reality of who they are — give them a break by destroying the myths. Perfect parents only exist on television. Respect your parents' rights to be imperfect. If you don't forgive them, then you are destined to repeat their failures. Loving them faults and all will free you to become better.

We must never be afraid to question our thoughts and emotions. Our lives depend on our willingness to truthfully examine the meditations of our hearts. When we find ourselves in new situations with the same old problems, we have to ask, "Where did this come from?" The answer we discover is the key that unlocks the door to the future.

## I Come

From generations of strong women, I come.

My grandmother's mother
Picked cotton in the fields.
Hands blistered, heart broken,
By wounds that never healed.

Grandma bore her children
By the light of the day.
By noon she planted her crops
For this is the strong woman's way.

From generations of strong women, I come.

Women so strong
We would not let them be weak.
Women so self-sufficient
A man's arms they could not seek.

Women so strong
Maybe you were afraid to hold them.
Women so scared of rejection
That all they could do was scold men.
From this I come.

Women whose nights
Were moistened by hot tears.
Women whose days
Turned into lonely, giving years.

Women so consumed
By their need to give to others.
Women called friends,
But never lovers.
From this I come.

The shoulder I cried on
So often needed a friend.
And from the lessons I have learned —
Now I send.

To my daughters, I send strength
That is not afraid to cry.
I send a belief in God's love
That will keep your dreams alive.

I send you wisdom and integrity
Knowledge and love of self.
Freedom to be who you are
Not an image from someone else.

I send you my heart,
My unique femininity.
I send you true womanhood,
Your right to be free.

Be young in your youth
Seasoned with grace when your life's sun sets.
In all of your giving
Don't be afraid to get.

Don't be a myth
Be an extraordinary womb-man.
Don't live on a pedestal
That can't be touched by human hands.

I promise to be a model.
A map that shows the way.
I promise to rewrite the lines
That "fate" wanted me to play.

From strong women I come
To strong women I send.
This is the generation
Where the loneliness...Ends.

> "INTIMIDATION WILL CEASE WHEN
> YOU REALIZE THAT WE *ALL*
> STRUGGLE WITH ISSUES!"

## CHAPTER 15
## THE COMMON DENOMINATOR

### EVERYBODY'S GOT THEM....

I love issues! I don't like having them, but I like the fact that I am not alone with mine. The one thing I know about every person I meet before we even start a conversation is that they have issues. Time will tell what they are, but I know they are there. Intimidation ceases when you recognize that you don't have to impress anyone because they struggle just like you do.

Sometimes issues are a product of our culture or family background. Sometimes they are imposed on us by society. I believe that many of the issues facing women are the result of society's definitions. Career women are respected, but if they're too smart there's a name for them. Women who have chosen to stay at home are sacrificing, but if they enjoy it too much there's a name for them too. We just can't seem to catch a break.

## I'M EVERY WOMAN — NOT

Femininity has a purpose, which is often misunderstood. Men who can't appreciate a woman's softness abuse it, and those who can't understand her unique strength, vilify it. Many find it hard to comprehend how the same woman who makes cutthroat million-dollar business deals can be reduced to tears by baby shampoo commercials. Woman's ability to be sensitive and yet display the strength of steel is mystifying.

Women can be so many things because God designed them to be both a reflection of His strength and His love. Unfortunately, women are often made to feel as if they must choose between these two expressions of their nature. This need to choose sometimes leads to what I call defeminization, or the loss of the feminine soul.

First, let me clarify what femininity is not. Femininity is not abandoning the good sense that God gave you so that you can fit someone else's definition of what a woman should be. Nor is it wearing outfits that emphasize your physical assets while you do nothing to improve the quality of your mind. Not at all. Femininity is about a woman's ability to be intelligent and logical while maintaining her capacity to be nurturing and intuitive. It is being able to ask for help when needed, but knowing that you have the strength to make it if help doesn't come.

Sociologists and scientists debate why men and women are different. Some believe it is the socialization process and others believe it to be biochemical. I tend to believe that our differences are a mixture of both factors working together. Regardless of why men and women differ, the fact is that they do.

We need to recognize that balance and harmony is the product of respecting and accepting these differences between the sexes. Unfortunately, we have been conditioned to think of men and women complementing each other solely in the context of romantic relationships. But the truth is that every social institution benefits when men and women express their uniqueness.

A woman playing her part doesn't mean taking dictation from a man. It means that we embrace women's unique ways of looking at things because it brings something new and different to the table. I am disheartened when I meet and talk to women who have been so battered and scarred by events that they do not appreciate their own value. The only thing that saddens me more is a woman who hides her true self because others cannot value her. Everyone has issues, but make sure the ones that you have are your own. Dealing with yourself is a full time job — you don't have the time or the energy to get caught up in someone else's mess.

### Bittersweet Sistah

Hands on your hips,
Attitude on your shoulder.
Cynical replies gracing your lips
Like a cancer-filled nicotine stick
You are a Bittersweet Sistah.

On your guard, on your own.
Got money to pay your bills,
Don't need nobody...
Just want to be left alone.

Laughing loud at the parties,
Your voice has got to be heard,
Got a right to your opinion.
Are you hurting? Absurd!!
Oh no, not you my Bittersweet Sistah!

Trying so hard to defend yourself,
Put your femininity on the shelf.
Exchanged it so you could equal a man
Not knowing your sensitivity
Has a power that is part of God's plan.

Since day one, you've had to do for yourself.
Couldn't depend on anyone else.
The day's been long and the knocks have been hard.
Sometimes nobody listened,
Nobody but God.

Am I talking to you?
Oh yes, I think so.
Pain has you stunted,
But it's time for you to grow.

Forget those hurts.
Cast down those pains.
Be refreshed by God's love,
Like flowers fed by the rain.

You are all woman,
Creative and unique.
Life and power in every word you speak.

Phenomenal and special
Deserving of love
Rise above your circumstances —
Find the peace you've been dreaming of.

'Cause I don't want to see you no more,
With your hands on your hips.
Attitude on your shoulder.
Negativity on your lips.
I don't want to call you my Bittersweet Sistah.

"INSECURITY IN SOMEONE ELSE'S
SUCCESS IS A SURE SIGN THAT YOU STILL
DON'T KNOW WHO YOU ARE!"

CHAPTER 16
BRING OUT THE BEST

## SISTER FRIENDS

When going through life's ups-and-downs, nothing compares to the companionship of a "sister-friend." She is the girlfriend you can call after midnight who talks to you as though it is the most natural thing in the world to carry on a conversation at three o'clock in the morning. When you tell her your secrets, you don't have to worry about them circling among your closest friends. She guards your frailties as if they were her own. She's the one you split the pint of ice cream with so you only get half the fat, and even though her Saturday nights are filled with *Good Times* reruns, she is more than willing to let you drone on and on about the new man in your life. Most important, your girlfriend knows you. She knows how you sound when something is on your mind, and she is not fazed by your quirky moods. If you have found a friend like this, hold on to her because she is a precious resource.

## THE ISSUE OF INSECURITY

While relationships between women can be spiritually enriching and satisfying, when women don't get along the "cattiness" can be devastating. Some women spend their lives competing with others. Driven by the dynamic duo of jealousy and insecurity, they have not learned to support each other without feeling intimidated. Instead they derive their esteem from comparing themselves with others. Some people aren't happy unless they drive the nicest car, make the most money, or everyone else thinks they're the best. True success cannot be measured by comparing yourself to someone else's standards, but can only be experienced by pushing yourself to reach your personal best. You will only enjoy contentment and personal success when you have learned that someone else's happiness is not a threat to yours.

## TOO MUCH TIME ON THEIR HANDS

Have you ever watched a poised woman pass a group of friends, and as she walks by one of them whispers (some are rude enough to get loud), "Oh, she thinks she's so cute!" I ask you, what is she supposed to think about herself? Why should she feel bad about being who she is? If she's not putting anyone down, what's the problem?

The real problem is not the sister. The problem lies in others' perceptions of themselves. Insecure people aren't happy with themselves, so they find contented people intimidating. This sense of inferiority often manifests in the form of backbiting and slander. I am amazed at the great comfort and ease that some can take in criticizing and judging others.

If you have time to analyze and discuss others' faults, then you are neglecting your own personal development. Though we must be aware of the positives and negatives of those around us, we should not spend our time gloating over the issues that we don't have. Instead, our words should be constructive and motivated by love. So before you get ready to send a wrecking crew to someone else's character — make sure your house is in order. If you use that as the criteria, I guarantee you won't have the time to go meddling in others' business. You will be too preoccupied with your own.

## WHAT WISE WOMEN DO

A secure woman knows how to love others and herself at the same time. She is not afraid to look in the mirror and compliment herself. She doesn't wait for someone else's validation, because she knows that placing your worth in another person's opinion can potentially make you their victim. You must learn to praise yourself so that when someone else gets recognition you don't think they are stealing something from you. We have bought into the hogwash that it is wrong to say positive things about ourselves, but true humility is saying about yourself and others what God has already said.

Even the closest of friends may experience times of jealousy and comparison. It's natural. But you must protect your friendship at all costs. Rejoice for your girlfriend's achievements with the same enthusiasm that you rejoice for yours. If God made it happen for her, then the same can happen for you. No one can take your place, so when you see others moving forward, don't feel like you have to rush to get there with them. Your blessings are reserved under your name. You will get there as you help others reach their destinations.

## Work It Girl, You Go!

Unashamed of who you are,
Not afraid to let others know
Your hopes, dreams and desires
You work it girl! You go!

You hold your head up high,
While refusing to put others down.
You're too busy pursuing destiny
To spread the next girl's business around town.

So secure in God's love
That you can let me be myself.
So joyful in your purpose,
You're not afraid to help someone else.

You think you're all that
And you think that I am too.
You're a woman who's defined herself,
Baby, I'm scared of you!

Not afraid to be lace and satin,
But facing life with determination of steel.
Your words flow with strength and wisdom,
You go girl! Keep it real!

Some don't understand you,
Because they don't understand themselves.
But you don't let that bother you —
Self-contentment...now that's your wealth.

Reaching for all you've ever dreamed of
What killed others made you grow.
I'm filled with pride each time I see you,
You work it girl! You go!

"DANCE WHEN THE MUSIC STOPS.
COLOR OUTSIDE THE LINES. DO
SOMETHING DIFFERENT EVERY DAY
TO REMIND YOURSELF THAT YOU
CAN CHANGE!"

## CHAPTER 17
## BEHIND THE MASK

### 24-HOUR DRAMA

Can you imagine working all day, every day? Nonstop.
Impossible, you say? Not so? Some people do it all the time.
They spend all day working on being someone other than who
they really are. They have perfected and crafted images that
keep them isolated from the real world and genuine involve-
ment. I know this because I once lived under a carefully con-
structed image. Day in and day out, I acted the part of the
completely self-sufficient woman and denied my needs for
others. Like some women put on makeup, I "put on" the
facade of self-assurance every morning. I made it clear that I
didn't need anybody!

In isolation, I let my hurts and pains fester into full-blown
bitterness, which often manifested itself in cynicism and sar-
castic cutting remarks. My pretense of independence required

no real vulnerability with friends, and therefore allowed very little accountability in my relationships. I rarely asked my friends for anything because I was afraid to confront my own needs.

## FORCED INTO RETIREMENT

This constant pretense drained me, and as I began H.E.A.L.I.N.G.™, I found it difficult to distinguish the real me from the image. What was really my temperament and which behaviors had I adopted in order to protect myself? The line between who I really was and who others perceived me to be was blurred. I soon realized that I was trapped in a role that I had created and others were comfortable with me playing.

Who are you acting for? Who do they say you are? Who have you become out of necessity and as a response to the demands of the world around you? Because it is human nature, people will attempt to deal with you in ways that are most comfortable for them. We all do it. But your responsibility is to know who you are. If you live for the approval of others, always conforming to expectations, you will miss out on what you really want.

## STAGE MAKEUP

Several years ago, I attended a conference with a group of peers. (By this point, my facade of being reserved and conservative was perfected.) I remember feeling older than everyone else, even though we were all in the same age group. I watched with longing as they played games, danced and enjoyed the music and good food. My facial expression was one of disinterest, yet inside I felt prisoner to the image that I had constructed. I felt trapped behind the fifteen pounds of excess weight that invaded my body. I felt like I was sitting at a feast but couldn't eat. I excused myself from the party and rushed to my hotel room to pour my thoughts into my journal. I searched for the words to capture my feelings. What was I feeling? I realized that I was afraid to be myself. I feared others would not accept me. Yet I wanted to forget who I was supposed to be and just be who I wanted to be!

As I journaled, the words of a friend who once compared me to a butterfly trapped in a jar came back to me. That night while the others enjoyed themselves, I lay in bed taunted by the sounds of their celebration. I wanted to return to the party, but somehow I couldn't move. Instead, I remained in my room, sentenced to the prison of my self-created role.

## Jarred Butterfly

Like a lump of hardened clay,
The jarred butterfly stood unmoved.
Wings folded by her side,
Body stiff like an on-duty soldier.

No one could see, no one knew
That her wings were brightly painted
With the color of life's rainbow.
Because she had kept their beauty hidden from sight.

No one knew that she could fly,
That she could soar amongst the clouds
And dance with the wind.

Someone had misunderstood her purpose.
They thought that she had been created
For their joy alone.
So they captured her and locked her in a plain glass jar.

Like a painting or a doll
They placed the jar on the shelf,
Punched holes in the lid,
And left her....

Sometimes, the jar was moved from the shelf
And placed on the windowsill in the sun.
The little butterfly could see the world.
The world she longed to fly in.

The sun's light would catch
The orange, red and yellow hues
That adorned her body.
Then she would spread her wings.

She would beat them against the confines of the glass.
She would strike them against the hole-ridden lid
That hindered her flight.
She would flap and flap,
Beating and beating until exhausted.
Then she would give up.

So no one knew that she could fly,
That she could soar amongst the clouds
And dance with the wind.

Soon, the jar would be back in the shadows of the shelf.
At home once again
With the dolls and other lifeless objects.
And the little butterfly would surrender
To the definitions of her captor.

And worst of all...
She would forget that she could fly —
That she could soar amongst the clouds
And that she could dance with the wind!


## Message to the Butterfly

Rise, beautiful butterfly
And stretch out your wings.
Dance with the rhythm of life's song
Live out the freedom of your dreams.

Reach, precious butterfly
For the things that remain unseen.
Bask in the beauty of the sun
Rejoice in the melody freedom sings.

Hope, wondrous butterfly
In the strength of your Creator.
Be whom God has called you —
For you, there's nothing greater.

Fly, beautiful butterfly
Soar higher, higher and higher.
Forget all that is behind you
Feel the heat of destiny's fire.

Escape from the prison
Where disappointment tried to cage you.
Fly, majestic butterfly
Be all that God has made you!

> "NEVER TRUST ANOTHER PERSON
> TO DEFINE YOU. THEY WILL ONLY
> MEASURE YOUR WORTH BY YOUR
> CONVENIENCE TO THEM!"

## CHAPTER 18
## NOBODY KNOWS YOU!

### BEYOND CLASSIFICATION

We love labels! They help us organize and classify things. Once we've stuck a label on something, we know where to put it. We label file folders so we know where to quickly access information. We label little freezer bags so we can know what the green thing is in the back of the fridge. And, yes, we label people so we can know what to do with them.

Anyone who has more than one sibling knows exactly what I mean. People develop little identifiers to help commit a person to memory. You hear it at family reunions, "That's the smart one." "That's the pretty one." "That's the one they better watch." I think we enjoying labeling people because it is so much easier to label and make assumptions than it is to get to know the real person. Labeling food is one thing, but labeling people and developing fixed and unchangeable ideas about them is nothing short of dangerous.

I am always amused when people tell me, " I know you." It makes me want to laugh. I do have friends and family who know my tastes, habits and philosophies so well that I can trust them to adequately represent my viewpoints or pick up a shirt at the mall they think I'd like. But no one has understood the full sum and total of the complexities that compose me. All human beings are in constant emotional evolution. Everyday things are changing and impacting our lives, requiring that we make adjustments and changes.

When you meet someone and assume that because of their skin color, economic status or genderyou have figured them out, you are doing yourself and the other person a disservice. It is an insult to a person's uniqueness to reduce them to a simple formula in your mind.

Be careful when you come across people who approach you formulaically. People will try to adjust you to fit a neat little package in their minds, but don't conform to it. Every time someone attempts to change you and trespass against your uniqueness, they are telling God that what he has authored is not good enough, or that you are too simple to bother giving full exploration. Don't be limited to a box in someone else's mind.

## NOT PART OF THE CLIQUE

Let me be the first to warn you that standing up for yourself doesn't always win you fans, but it does get you respected. Assert your uniqueness. People who can't accept you for who you are don't deserve or need to be an intimate part of your life. "going along to get along" makes things easier for everyone else, but it kills you slowly.

Standing up for yourself shouldn't be motivated by a contrary attitude, but rather self-love. If self-love is the motivation, then that love will extend to the possible offenders. In your relationships, show a little grace. Remember that people come into your life fully loaded with issues of their own. They need a little time, just as you do. Have the wisdom to look past imperfections and see the treasure underneath. It's what you'd want someone to do for you.

## Young Black Man

Young Black Man
Stand tall, be strong
I know your road has been weary
And the journey has been long.

For centuries enslaved,
And for decades denied,
Don't bow to the pressure
Lift your head up — have pride.

You are more than you know,
Young Black Man you are —
Your strength is supernatural
Your beauty, radiant like stars.

They thought they knew you,
They shamed you with lies.
Called you $\frac{3}{5}$ of a person —
A lesser man would have died.

Though others desire
To script your destiny.
Erase the lines on history's page —
Be the author of your dreams.

They called you stupid —
Tell them they lied.
They called you a failure
Tell them, "that failure died."

Hold your head up,
Stick your chest out,
Square your shoulders,
Be Strong!

Keep moving,
Keep striving,
Keep pushing,
Hold On!

I love to see power
Burning in your eyes.
Strength in your jawbone
And purpose in your stride.

Be you caramel, chocolate
Café au lait or tan
You are awesome and beautiful,
My brother — the young black man!

*H:*   Help While You're Hurting

*E:*   Enjoy Life's Process

*A:*   Accept and Anticipate Change

*L:*   Let Go...

*I:*   Itemize Your Issues and Images

*N:*   **Navigate Your Needs**

*G:*   Grow with Gratitude

# STRATEGY SIX

*Navigate Your Needs*

Vision and discipline keep us from giving up what we want most for what we want at the moment. Chaos enters our lives when we allow our wants and desires to drive our behaviors and relationships without the constraints of character. Navigating our emotional needs can be tricky. Needs carry an intensity — a thirst of sorts. Our desires can scream so loudly that it is difficult to make the right decisions. We must learn the balance between respecting our desires and serving our needs. Every one of us has the right to affection, affirmation and love in our lives. However, we must understand that all these things must obey certain guidelines before they come into our lives. Love cannot come into our lives attached to people who do not help us to grow and improve beyond our current situations. Affirmation cannot come through people who use their praise as a means of manipulation. Affection cannot come without boundaries, or it can turn into a possessiveness that diminishes the soul. We must examine our lives to make sure that we are navigating our emotional needs, rather than allowing our desires to drive us into dangerous territory.

There are conditions under which our needs and desires are to be filled. Enlist discipline and vision to help you

develop the patience needed to maturely handle the fulfill-
ment of your deepest desires. Time and patience reveal the
quality and character of everything — let them work in your
life to navigate your needs and reveal the real matters of your
heart.

> "MORAL CONSISTENCY IN TIMES
> OF LACK AND ABUNDANCE IS A TRUE
> SIGN OF CHARACTER AND MATURITY."

## CHAPTER 19
## WHEN HUNGER STRIKES

Our needs must exist within the constraints of vision and character. Outside of these, your mind and emotions will work against you and eventually place your integrity at risk. Need is like a child. It must have guidance, direction and discipline. Vision is the parent that provides these things.

True vision is submission to a set of principles and standards that govern your behaviors as you strive towards your goals. There are things that you must want to be, both emotionally and spiritually, in order to manage your needs. Your life must be larger than the present moment or you will make irrational decisions and act recklessly.

Ask anyone who has ever indulged in an affair. Their love for their family was forgotten and for a moment, they were caught up in whatever emotional needs the other person fulfilled in their lives. They did not think of the future. They didn't think of divorce or trying to raise their kids from two different homes. The only thought was immediate, short-term pleasure.

## THE ENDS DON'T JUSTIFY THE MEANS

In my own life, I have noticed a common thread running through most of my mistakes. It was using improper means to meet legitimate needs. Hunger is a valid need, but stealing is not the proper means of satisfying it. Without a higher set of principles in operation, you will do anything to meet your needs and you will not count the cost it has towards your future.

If there is any area in your life where need is so intense that you can barely see your blessings — watch out! You are on temptation's hit list. Temptation will tell you that you won't get caught, your needs will be satisfied, and what you are doing isn't so bad. It will cause you to rationalize your actions. It starts when you toy with an idea that you never seriously intended to act upon. It just makes you feel good to think about it.

Sometimes women don't get the type of appreciation and affirmation they desire at home. It isn't that they aren't loved, but that they don't hear the compliments they need to hear. Suddenly, at work someone notices them and showers them with compliments. This person notices a new dress and new hairdo. They notice and appreciate the hard work she does. Almost imperceptibly, her attitude towards work will change and she starts taking a little more care. It may begin with lunches, and then working a little later than necessary, and sometimes it can end up in bed. Temptation says, "You deserve whatever it is you need, so go ahead and take it!" But the temporary satisfaction that yielding to temptation brings is insignificant in comparison to the damage it can cause.

Temptation is not just sexual. It can be financial — you know that you can't afford that new big-screen TV, but you are too busy keeping up with your friends. So you get yourself into a world of debt that you are unprepared to handle. Temptation is multidimensional, but its ultimate goal is to get you to compromise your beliefs and values. All it takes is once for you to get caught and the rest of your life can be spent dealing with the consequences. I believe that we can recover from anything, but every decision bears a consequence that we must face.

## TRUSTING YOURSELF

The true damage of temptation is not what it costs others; it is what it costs your self. Submitting to temptation will cause you to doubt your own character and strength. You cannot act against your moral standards and principles without losing faith in yourself and the integrity of your word. You must be able to trust yourself more than you trust any other person. You must be your own best friend! You must be able to rely on and respect yourself. That is why it is so important that you keep your word. Failure to do so will cause you to feel as if you can't count on yourself. Though others may stand around and extol your virtues, when you know you are hiding something, you can't respect yourself. Self-respect is fundamental to true success in life.

## THE POWER OF AGREEMENT

You can't change what you have already done, but you can move forward into your future. What do you want out of life? What do you need out of life? These two areas must be in agreement. Don't give yourself the crutch of having a "weakness." You relinquish your power when you have ready excuses for doing what you know is wrong. You must discipline yourself to take the necessary actions towards your goals. Yes, you need affection, but it has to meet a certain set of standards. Yes, you need affirmation, but you must choose where it comes from. Remove yourself from anyone or anything that threatens to compromise your values.

## Temptation

Temptation comes to everyone,
To destroy what character builds
And the only question you need to ask is,
"Will I stand or yield?"

Offering promises of relief,
And momentary satisfaction.
The years invested to live your dreams,
Can be negated with just one action.

Temptation comes to lure you in,
With a slow, methodical dance.
But before you kiss its tempting lips
RUN...while you still have a chance!

Don't be foolish and
Consider yourself to be greater than you are.
For many have walked temptation's way
And been left with wounds and scars.

No need to search in foreign lands
When tracking this enemy's moves.
Its weapons lie much closer than that —
Look amongst what is common to you.

So next time your mind
Entertains the possible sensations.
Remember there's a death that lives in life,
And its name is Sweet Temptation.

So guard your heart and stay on track.
Its strength is found in what you lack.
What you give up, you can't get back.
Beware of Sweet Temptation!

"TO GET WHAT YOU NEED, YOU MUST
GIVE WHAT AND WHEN YOU CAN."

CHAPTER 20
ANALYZE THIS...PLEASE!

Need is powerful. A met need satisfies and produces happiness. An unmet need can create frustration and anger. At one point in my life, I was embarrassed by my need for human comfort and affection, but I could not deny my hunger and thirst for them when I was alone. Publicly, I appeared to have it all together. I was busy trying to have the answers for everyone else, but I had none for myself. I was so caught up in being "Dear Abby" that I didn't know how to ask for help. My denial of my needs made it acceptable for others to overlook them. Friends stopped asking the probing questions. In fact it wasn't unusual at all for me to hear comments like, "I know you're alright, so I won't even ask." Meanwhile, my world was crumbling and I didn't have enough strength to hold it all together. Needless to say I became angry with my friends for not seeing who, and where, I really was.

## BOUNDARIES

If you find yourself receiving treatment you don't deserve, or you think others negate your existence, think before you get angry. Stop and check yourself. Those around you may simply be following your lead. How have you have been dealing with your needs?

## MORSE CODE

Our loved ones aren't psychic, and it is rare to find individuals who can see behind your mask to find the real you. You are going to have to communicate what you want to others. I know it would be nice if they had it all figured out — but since you don't, why should they? Recently, a close friend of mine and I went through a particularly tough time in our relationship. If you were to ask him, he'd say he doesn't know what I'm talking about. But, to me our relationship was taking a turn for the worse. I felt undervalued and unappreciated. In our relationship it's not at all unusual for us to ask quick little favors of each other, but at some point I became resentful because I felt more favors were being asked than given. In hindsight, I realize that give and take will never be equal. There will be times when you give more than you take and vice versa.

Over time, I became extremely annoyed with all the little details and niceties that I felt he was overlooking. Little courtesies like walking me to my door or simply returning a phone call in a timely fashion seemed to be things that he couldn't do any longer. Eventually everything became a sore point between us. I was frustrated and despite my many attempts to explain my feelings, I could not get him to understand.

Then suddenly it hit me! It is true that on one level I was disappointed in my friend for not living up to my definitions of chivalry, but the intensity with which I felt undervalued had everything to do with me. Although I was yelling at him about things like not returning my calls, deep inside I was saying, "Help me to like me by making me feel valued." I had given up self-care and was making unfair demands on the friendship. I was asking him to do for me what I needed to do for myself.

## RECEIVING SIGNALS

In sharing your needs with family and friends, make it a point to remain sensitive to their needs as well. Author Mike Murdock often says, "What you make happen for others, God will make happen for you." Though you may have needs in your life, you should focus on finding where you can help meet the needs of others. Remember, you do have power. Someone can benefit from where you are strong, and in helping them, your needs can be met. Acknowledge your need, but recognize your power as well! Allow yourself to be a blessing to others, because when you meet needs you are allowing yourself to be the greatest reflection of God's love.

### I Need

Sometimes in midnight hours,
I lay helplessly on the floor.
And while others rest so peacefully,
I lay crying behind closed doors.

Kept awake by desires
That continue to go unfulfilled.
Growing weak in my spirit,
Time gnawing away at my will.

Waking me when what I need,
Is human love and sleep.
My mind asks the eternal question,
"What have I sown, that this is what I reap?"

I desire a better life,
But my lack just seems to taunt.
And though thankful for what I already have,
The voice I hear is want.

Wanting not for selfish reasons,
Not for lust, pride or greed.
Wanting because like everyone else...
I hunger, I thirst, I need.

A hunger so real that in sunshine,
It's a constant cloud of rain.
A thirst so life-threatening
It becomes actual physical pain.

Want so intense,
That it seems to grow and breed.
Want that seems to go ignored
And becomes frustration's seed.

I cannot help but ask myself,
Can God get a flower from this weed?
Will my deepest hope be satisfied, or
Will my life long friend be need?

Is this a call to greatness?
Do I have the strength to heed?
Can I see beyond the pain inside?
Can I see beyond my needs?

It costs much to be the fertile ground
From which others can live and feed.
But the price of vision
Is character watered by need.

"REAL LOVE GOES BEYOND REASONS."

CHAPTER 21

THE MODEL OF LOVE

Love and acceptance are human needs that are just as important to our well-being as food and shelter. The need to feel loved can be an ache that keeps you awake in the middle of the night. Even when we enjoy rich and satisfying relationships, we can experience times of restlessness. On the outside we appear to have it all, but inside we are discontented. What are we looking for? What is missing? More love, deeper love.

It has been said that God is love and love is God. It is said so often that it has become trivialized. But I dare you to explore the meaning of this statement. Turn it upside down, right side up, and inside out. Hold it up to the light and then feel it in the darkness. And once you think you understand it, start all over again. Because with all the searching and exploration you have done, you have only managed to touch the surface.

For those of you who feel alone and abandoned, who know that your quest is for love, stop searching. God is the love that you're looking for. He is too big to be locked up in someone's opinion of you. He is greater than your challenges. He is surrounding you, but the problem is that you have not yet realized that you are searching for Him.

You have tried to get to Him through someone else. You worked hard for straight A's in school trying to get Him from your parents; you gave your body out like free ice trying to cool the burning frustrations of your heart. You held on when you should've let go, trying to keep people from leaving you.

You can stop searching now; there is a place of rest. The love you are searching for cannot be found in people. It is higher and deeper than any love that you have ever known. Reflect upon God's goodness in your heart. Acknowledge what He has already done for you and know that if He has done this, He will do more! He loves you without reason and it is time for you to start loving yourself based on those same conditions! He is aware of all the good and the wrong that you have done. Guess what? He still loves you. He loves you enough to die for you, now love Him enough to live for Him.

You thought if you bought the Mercedes the void would be filled. When that didn't work, you bought the bigger model, but that didn't work either! Love is God and God can't be bought and then driven off the showroom floor. You can't buy His love; it is free.

God works through order and if you allow Him to, He will cause life to make more sense for you. Just receive God's love and your search will be over. The only thing left for you now is to explore its depths!

# In Spite of Love

I need a love that is unconditional,
With strength that lasts like time.
I need a love that is more than natural,
Something special, unique...divine.

I need a love that has no reasons,
One that is stronger than because.
What I really need in life is some of that
"In spite of" love...

"In spite of" sees beyond my faults,
And beholds what I can be.
"In spite of" knows that I can be better,
But still chooses to love only me.

"In spite of" knows that sometimes when I speak,
I can be hurtful and out of turn.
But, "in spite of" knows that my heart is right
And gives me room to grow and learn.

I cannot simply settle
For a love based on because...
If it is to last forever,
It must be "in spite of" love.

If love is because of reasons,
What would happen should the reasons change?
If love is because I make you happy,
Where will love go when I cause you pain?

I'm too old to believe in fairy tales,
But too young to give up my dreams.
I do believe that "in spite of" love
Finds those who understand the gift it brings.

Some say that I am asking a lot,
But I don't believe that is true.
Because "in spite of" love is not about us.
It is God loving me through you.

*H:* Help While You're Hurting

*E:* Enjoy Life's Process

*A:* Accept and Anticipate Change

*L:* Let Go...

*I:* Itemize Your Issues and Images

*N:* Navigate Your Needs

*G:* **Grow with Gratitude**

# STRATEGY SEVEN

## *Grow with Gratitude*

You will THRIVE! as you grow in your awareness and appreciation of your blessings. In order to grow with gratitude, you must shift your focus from your lack to your abundance. You must turn to your internal resources and be grateful to God that you have them. Be grateful for the small things because they will strengthen you as a person and increase your capacity for more. By choosing to be grateful, you shed a victim mentality. By shedding a victim mentality, you put yourself in a position to operate from a place of strength and power, a power you can use to make the changes that you know you need to make. A power you can use to get through the challenges and difficulties that you are facing. A power you can use to live and go beyond the confines of mere existence and push into *thriving*!

> "PEOPLE WHO OPPOSE YOU
> AND ATTEMPT TO BLOCK YOUR SUCCESS
> ARE JUST FOR WEIGHT LIFTING!"

## CHAPTER 22
## DESTINED TO WIN

Your destiny is a decision, and the decision is all yours. If you are allowing someone else's opinion of you or your situation to hinder your progress, you have given that individual entirely too much power. Are you avoiding certain places because "you know who" is there and you don't want to face them? Those tactics are for people who still build castles in the sandbox! The bottom line is this: you are responsible for the condition of your life!

People, situations and negative opinions will present you with every obstacle possible, but you must resolve to move forward. People may slow you down for a moment, but they cannot stop you altogether. You must refuse to surrender your spirit to your adversaries. Instead, you must use them for your good. Muscle is built as it works against an opposing force. People who oppose you and attempt to block your success are just for weight lifting!

## IT'S JUST AN INGREDIENT IN THE SOUP

Failure is a part of life and a necessary ingredient in success. You are not qualified to succeed until you have withstood the disappointment of failure. Failure in your life should only serve as a means of identifying the things that need to be corrected. Failure is not the end of the book; it is only a sign that you need to start a new chapter!

Instead of investing energy in self-pity, take the time to analyze the factors that contributed to failure, so that you don't repeat them when you try again. Thank failure for the lesson it has taught you about life. Crying time is over. Let every setback in life be only a set up for something that is about to blow everybody's mind!

### You Can't Stop Me!

You can't stop me,
No matter how hard you try.
I've decided to keep on living.
It's not time for me to die.

This pain is for a moment,
But the glory produced will last.
Winter is just a season.
This trouble came to pass.

You can't stop me,
No matter how set your plans.
My destiny is my decision.
The power is not in your hands.

The future is in what I believe,
It is not in what I see.
So I'm serving notice to hard times.
You can't stop me.

No longer can I lie here,
As fear rapes my mind.
I've got to reach for a better life
And leave negative things behind.

For too long, I have placed my hopes
In someone else's speech.
But my words shape my existence
And bring my desires within reach.

You can't stop me!
Because you don't have that much control.
You are just an obstacle
To be overcome as I reach my goals.

So fight me.
Spite Me.
Backbite Me.
Pursue Me.
One thing for sure, you can't go through me!
If you don't like it —
So what? Sue me.
But you can't stop me!

So go ahead, and do your dirt.
Lay your trap,
But it won't work.
It may sting and
It may hurt.
But you can't stop me!

> "CHANGE YOUR LIFE
> ONE THANK YOU AT A TIME!"

## CHAPTER 23
## GOOD HOME TRAINING

Failure to appreciate what you have because it isn't exactly what you wanted will create smallness of spirit. Even more than that, it will rob you of the beauty that exists around you right now. I know so many people who are frustrated because they aren't making the kind of money they think they should be, but not once have they stopped to appreciate the things that money cannot buy. Developing a grateful attitude for even the smallest of things will empower you.

Before my father passed away, so many things seemed to matter. I was frustrated and angry about being single. I was sick of my job and I was obsessed with my weight. I can't tell you the multitude of tears I shed over things that were insignificant. When my father died, I gained a sense of clarity about life that I'd never had before. Suddenly, I realized that being single is not a curse. It is a blessing, just a different blessing than marriage. I realized that weight isn't as important as good health. Though I'd like to be a smaller size, I have health and for that I am grateful. When people with a smallness of spirit attack you and attempt to smudge your character, be grateful. Be grateful that you don't have that smallness of spirit.

Be grateful for little things! How many times do you thank God for your ability to care for yourself? I know that to more "sophisticated" thinkers my attitude may seem simplistic and unrefined. But I have found that life is simple, and we make it complex. I am determined to be grateful because when gratitude courses through my veins, I am energized. Be thankful for your family, be thankful for your health, be thankful for opportunity, and be thankful for human kindness! These are the things we cannot do without in life, yet these are the things we overlook and neglect the most. Every day, think of something to be thankful to God for and throughout the day keep it at the forefront of your mind. I guarantee you; your life will change because gratitude affects the way we see everything that comes into our path.

### Every Day

Every day I think of you
And what you meant to me.
I still can't believe you've crossed the line
Between time and eternity.

If anyone had told me
That today you would only live in my mind.
I would have thought them crazy,
For I thought that I had time.

In life you were always there for me,
A companion and a friend.
And in my youthful lack of sight,
I thought "we" would never end.

Every day I remember
The things that made you unique.
And every day to God I pray
For the answers my heart seeks.

How could one so full of life
Be torn from by my side?
So much of what I have achieved
I did because your eyes showed pride.

Public and private tears
Have burned and blurred my eyes.
And many nights I've fallen asleep,
Asking the eternal "Whys?"

Why of all the pains in life
Is this one I have to know?
And when things were finally going right,
Why did you have to go?

Why not someone else?
Why couldn't you be a miracle too?
Why not someone I didn't know?
Why did it have to be you?

But there is a silver lining
Although I wish there was no cloud.
And even though pain rapes my heart
There is a truth that sorrow can't shroud...

I would rather know this pain of loss,
Than the loss of not knowing you.

In memory of Willie James Scott, Willie Anthony Williams
and Hasson David Benjamin, Sr.

> "YOU ARE DESTINED TO WIN!
> THE QUESTION IS, WILL YOU TAKE
> THE JOURNEY?"

CHAPTER 24
THE JOURNEY

We have come to the end of our strategies, but I encourage you to proceed to the **Thrive! H.E.A.L.I.N.G.™ Journaling Guide** that follows. Journaling played a crucial role in my H.E.A.L.I.N.G.™ process. I pray that *Thrive!* has proven itself to be a worthwhile investment for you. The days ahead of us are rich and each new day can bring us understanding that we didn't have before.

There are some people who thought I would never finish this book and that it would always be something that I just talked about, but they were wrong! There is always someone who is willing to believe negative things about you. Just make sure that you are not one of them!

I thank everyone who had a part in my completing this project. Love made this possible. I would also like to thank my enemies for this book as well. My enemies are not people, though they often use people. My enemies are fear, discouragement, negative thinking, and anything else that attemps to hinder the completion of God's work in my life. So to my enemies I say: If you did not challenge me, I may never have known how good God is! If you did not doubt me, I may never have known true faith! If you did not attempt to hinder me with your "No's," I might never have known the power of God's eternal "Yes!"

I wrote this book with the hope that I could encourage you. I want you to see yourself making it through every midnight. I want you to see yourself dancing in the sunlight. I want you to grow rich and dig deep into your wealth of experience. It is time for you to do more than survive — it's time for you to THRIVE!

### Fierce!

Fierce means bad.
Not bad meaning bad,
But bad meaning good.
Fierce means
On point
On time
Revolutionary
In your face
Jump Back,
Because you can't touch this.

And now, as the definition ends
Let my melodic, free-flowing verse begin.

Not I,
But He,
And together, We
Can destroy the "im" in impossibilities.

Not Me
But Him,
Won't sink
We'll swim
Through the seas of life's adversities.

Bring challenge,
Bring pain
He makes it all to my gain
And no weapon formed shall prosper.

Yeah, I'm talking loud
I've got a right to be proud.
Because the God in me is Fierce.

You Huff, You Puff
And you talk real rough,
But you'll choke
On that talk your smokin'.

Down talkin' my wealth
With your negative self.
Overcome me?
You must be jokin'.
Give it all you've got
Pull out all the stops.
On my behalf
He'll show Himself strong.

You thought you silenced my song,
But you've got it all wrong.
Because the God in me is Fierce.

I may stumble, may fall
Sometimes it's hard to stand tall.
I'm cast down,
But I'm never forsaken.

You throw shadows
Called "fear"
But the truth is clear,
I'm not destroyed, I've only been shaken.

Draw knives of contention
And guns of division,
But I'm sheltered in His mighty hands.

Throw rocks —
They'll turn to sand.
And as the dust clears,
Watch me stand!
Because the God in me is Fierce.

My God is bad.
Not bad meaning bad,
But bad meaning good.
He is on point
On time
Revolutionary
In your face
Jump Back
Bow down
Fierce!

He stands for me
And I stand in Him.

Haven't you heard?
He's the Truth and the Word.
Don't you know?
That the God in me is Fierce?

**T h r i v e !**

In all the dirt
Through all the lies
Though I can't even swim
I flow with the tide
Because like the sun in the morning,
My strength will rise
I'll do more than get by
I will Thrive!

I will fall down and get back up
I'll swallow the lessons from life's bitter cup
When offenses come, my joy won't get stuck
I'll suffer the blows that I've been too slow to duck.

When my hope faints
And my joy is weak
When my spirit is weary
And I can't even speak
I'll look to the hills,
Until the cavalry arrives
Rest assured, I won't die
I will Thrive!

Thrive means to live abundantly,
It's to hope in the heart for what my eyes can't see.
It's to push the thousandth time on the unopened door
It's to try it again, though I've tried it before.

It's to get past folks' issues, both yours and mine
To pierce past the clouds and find the silver line.
It's to march to my life's beat and keep my own time.
It's to love when hate is plentiful,
Cause I've got God's sunshine.

It's to give when I have nothing
Because I know I've got it all.
It's to be big in my spirit when I want to be small.
It's to rejoice for no reason that others can see
It's to live out the potential that richly dwells in me.

No matter what life wants to give
I will not expire — I have decided to live!
Where is the challenge?
I'm not trying to hide.
No matter how weighed down,
I'm in for the whole ride.

So don't talk to me about someone else,
I'm too busy working on myself.
Don't tell me how it is too hard
I'll take it inch by inch to finish out the yard.

Don't tell me it's hopeless,
Because I'll know that you've lied.
I am destined to win —
I am destined to Thrive!

## "LOVE IS THE REAL TREASURE OF LIFE!"

## SPECIAL DEDICATIONS

Growing up, my mother made being a woman look so easy. I never guessed how hard it would be to make ends meet, to stand strong and be fair in this world. I never guessed that sometimes it would take all of your strength, just to keep going.

My mother is my hero and the more I know about her, the greater she becomes in my eyes. Not because she's perfect or always says the right things. Because, believe me, she isn't and she doesn't (there are moments when all she seems to say is the wrong thing). Like your mother and all mothers, she can be a test of the nerves. But I've lived long enough to know that perfection isn't the foundation for heroism, it is courage — the courage to do and be something different, even when it is not always the easiest thing to do.

I have not always appreciated the person my mother is. In fact there was a time when I resented her. I didn't like that she was a little too strict and wouldn't let me have my way. I didn't like that she always seemed to have a particular standard that wouldn't let me do what everyone else was doing. For some

years, she was just this person standing between me and every-
thing I wanted. As a child I could not wait to become a grown
up!

With age has come wisdom, and now I see. Now I see her
and recognize the person she is — and in my unbiased opin-
ion she is flawed, but oh so remarkable! My mother is one of
the greatest gifts God has ever given me. Life without her
would be colorless. The wealth that she has given me may not
be visible to the naked eye, but when I hold my inheritance up
in the face of the trials of life, it is clear to me that the lessons
Mama has taught me are priceless!

## That's Mama to Me

Collard greens steaming, macaroni and cheese bubbling,
Cornbread browning and sweet potato pie
That melts in your mouth,
Like butter on plump roasted corn...
That sounds like Mama to me.

I can see her now in that hot and stuffy kitchen.
Wearing that housedress I wanted to throw away.
Back door open, and that little three-speed fan
That only blew stale heat.

Beads of sweat anointing her arms and forehead
As she weaves the cloth of love
That holds my family together.
A cloth so strong and sturdy
That I have wrapped myself in its security
As I've faced life's midnight hours.

Now I know some folks would have you believe that heroes
Change in phone booths and fly through the air
With a letter of the alphabet across their chest.
But not me...

You want to talk about amazing?
Mama could talk on the phone, wash clothes,
Stir a cake batter, cook a good meal on that four-eyed,
Only-two-eyes-working stove
And still have time to catch me
Before I could sneak out the front door.

If I ever thought Mama was special,
It was on Sunday mornings.
There she was, calling us, telling us to get ready.
Didn't she know I had prayed already?

Yes, I did — I prayed she would leave me alone
And let me stay home.
Didn't she know that it didn't take two hours
For me to get dressed?
I am sure she knew, but that didn't stop Mama!
Every Sunday, eleven thirty service.
Everybody else, including the preacher,
Showed up at eleven.
But Mama didn't care; we'd walk in there late.

What would make a woman deal with the hassle of
Hardheaded children, dragging feet and pouting lips?
I used to wonder about Mama.
How could she clap so loud? Sing so loud? Rejoice so loud?
Didn't we just get on her nerves five minutes ago?

But she knew something, or should I say someone?
She knew that one day we would need Him.
She knew that life would one day disappoint us
And threaten to almost break us.
But Mama also knew that if we could see Him in her,
We too would walk on water in life's storms.

On Mother's Day some write of roses, tea parties,
Dainty cakes, afternoon drives
And trips to faraway places.
Of these things I have none.

But in abundance I have: a shoulder to lean on, hope
eternal, friend unfailing, freely giving, persevering, arms
securing and love unending...

THAT'S MAMA TO ME!

> "MEMORY REHEARSED CAN BE
> MORE POWERFUL THAN YOUR
> PRESENT REALITY."

## MEMORIES

Memories connect who we were to who we are. They are moments that stand outside the boundaries of time and live forever. Feelings and sensations merge the past with the present and leave you suspended in the very moment the memory was created.

For me, nothing creates memories better than music. The soulful crooning of Sam Cooke, Marvin Gaye and The O'Jays set the background for some of my best memories. These songs played in the background when I fell in love for the very first time.

The year was 1976, and I was five years old. The object of my affections was an intelligent, charismatic and good-looking man. He had an infectious smile and sense of humor. His laugh was better than any song, and like music it would run through my heart and flow into my feet, making me want to dance.

He was 25 years my senior, but our age difference did not matter. Oh no, what we had was real love. We didn't even need words to express our feelings. We would sit together for hours, listening to music. He would dance with me at times, and then at others he would serenade me. He was the man of my dreams...Daddy!

Sometimes I ask myself what made me love him as I did. There were so many things that I loved about him that it is difficult to say what endeared him to me most. I loved his laugh because it secured me. As a child I felt that as long as he was laughing, then all was in its place. I loved the way his neck would jerk as he grunted to himself. I knew this meant that he was thinking about something humorous, but not meant to be shared. If I had to choose one thing, it would have to be his backward country sayings that made me love him most.

As a child, I thought my father was "out of touch," but as I grow older I discover that his words were rich in wisdom. The speeches I once tolerated are now the source of my strength. For example, when I would do something inconsiderate he would simply say, "You'll see it again." In other words, both right and wrong have a way of coming back to you. My passionately expressed juvenile opinions were never disputed, instead he would simply nod his head and say, "Life will teach you what you need to know."

I now appreciate the insights my Father shared with me about life and human nature. Though life's events can sometimes surprise me, his words of wisdom have prepared me to face any challenge.

Music was an integral part of our relationship. It was our way of having a conversation without saying a word. It was our way of knowing that our father/daughter connection was special. When I left home for college, later moving to New York City, we would call each other and share music over the phone. To my father I owe my love of music and my ability to think and see things from a perspective other than my own.

He taught me about life in little phrases that are so easy to remember and hard to forget. The greatest thing a parent can teach a child is how to live without them. I am thankful to Pops for the words of wisdom that help me to go on even though he is gone.

## Music Memories

One o'clock in the morning,
I can't even rest.
Sam Cooke is crooning,
Emotions rising up in my chest.

Wipe my sleepy eyes,
My little feet hit the ground.
Head to the living room
Where Pops is getting down.

Sitting at the old turntable,
Spinning that forty-five.
Daddy is lost in the sixties,
I see memories filling his eyes.

"Hey, baby girl," he says
As he clears his favorite chair.
"Come spend some time with Daddy."
"Got some good music I want to share."

He would close his eyes and listen
To the be-bop melodies,
Daddy would sing that music
And forget all about lil' me.

We'd take a stroll on the boardwalk
Listening to the Supremes Symphony.
Then we'd spend some time with Nat King Cole.
Just my Daddy and lil' ole me.

Daddy would talk of good old days
Days before my time.
Days when music was simple
And lyrics did more than rhyme.

Hour after hour,
He would play those records till they smoked.
Every once in a while,
He'd crack a little joke.

Four o'clock in the morning,
Sleep is calling me.
But I'd rather be with Daddy
Making music memories.

My eyes would get heavy
And my head would begin to fall.
He'd ask me if I were sleepy
And I would lie and say,
"Not at all."

But my little sleepy body
Would betray my every lie.
And I would drift off to a dreamland.
Listening to sounds of days gone by.

# H.E.A.L.I.N.G.™
# Journaling Guide

> ## "MAKE THE ISSUES OF YOUR LIFE PLAIN
> ## BY WRITING THEM DOWN."

## INTRODUCTION

My pen was my salvation at a time when I could not adequately or confidently verbalize my emotions. I found a connection with writing, and it was my secret weapon. With my pen, I literally chopped away at the negative thoughts that once held my mind captive. I could always trust it to be a light that helped me to navigate the darkness that held me back from the answers I needed to begin to love, accept and value myself. This brief section cannot do justice to the power of journaling and its many benefits. Instead, it is intended to be an introduction to the possibilities that are awaiting you when you began the joy of self-discovery through writing. I believe that writing about your emotions, examining them and then acting upon what you learn can radically change your life. Just think, you are only a piece of paper and pen away from thriving!

## A "STUART LITTLE" LESSON

The natural world can give great insight into our emotional and spiritual lives. Lessons surround us everyday, but in our hectic, deadline-driven lives we often miss them. As I've said before, it is quite often the things we don't like that lead us to another level of knowledge.

I once learned a lesson from mice and believe me when I say that nothing can send me scrambling quicker than the appearance of one. I will never forget the night I walked into my bedroom, turned on the light and screamed in horror as a mouse scurried across the floor. I couldn't believe it was in my home! My territory was invaded. Of course I had no real reason to fear, as the mouse was more afraid of me than I was of it. But my emotions couldn't hear logic as I pleaded with my brother-in-law to come and get me!

The next day, the management office sent over an exterminator to check every square inch of my apartment, including my pipes and radiators. But he could not find the mouse's entrance. He put out some poison and glue traps and within a couple days we had caught a few. I didn't see anything for months and then one day...I came in the house after a hard day's work to a dead mouse on my floor. This problem persisted for two years, on and off.

Finally, I demanded a new apartment and management's response was to send over their best maintenance men who removed my dishwasher, sink and cabinets. Moving all of these things, they found the holes! For two years, they had been sending over the exterminator and other people who took perfunctory glances without moving anything to find the source of the problem.

Like those maintenance men who wanted the easy task of just glancing around, many of us don't want to delve into the dark corners of our emotions. We want problems to just magically fade away. But I've got news for you — if you don't find the entry point of the issues in your life, they will continue to persist. They will rear their ugly heads at the most inopportune and inconvenient moments.

Journaling can help you move everything out of the way and renovate. It will help you to find the little holes that let in tiny things that end up becoming huge and doing a lot of damage. It will help you to uncover what would otherwise remain hidden. But you must be willing to be ruthless with your emotions as you journal towards H.E.A.L.I.N.G.™ In using the word ruthless, I'm not advising you to ignore, belittle, or be callous towards your emotions. I mean you must be willing to face them head on and pray, think, cry and plan your way through to victory.

The following is merely a brief outline. For more journaling resources and our *Thrive! Today* newsletter, which features monthly journaling exercises, log on to www.butterflyworks.net. Based on the H.E.A.L.I.N.G.™ strategies discussed within the main section of the book, here are some exercises that focus on taking practical steps to help you thrive in your life.

## JOURNALING OVERVIEW

### WHAT IS JOURNALING?

Journaling is the art of reflection and expression through the process of uninhibited writing. It is the chance to write your story and quite possibly script your emotional future. Through connecting to your deepest fears, thoughts, hopes and desires, you are able to deal with the true issues of your life.

### HOW DO A DIARY AND JOURNAL DIFFER?

- Diary — focuses more on outside events/records the activities of the day
- Journal — focuses on capturing the thoughts and emotions experienced throughout the day

## TYPES OF JOURNALS AND THEIR FUNCTIONS:

- Dream journal — record your dreams
- Goals and vision journal — set your future goals
- Photo journal — use pictures to illustrate your life
- Video/audiotape journal — record family events and every-day interactions

Your journal is your book. It is a place of refuge, where you can be open and honest about your feelings. Journaling is a way of tapping into the "hidden man of the heart" to gain a better understanding of what drives you.

## WHY JOURNAL?

There are three key benefits to journaling:

### 1. Health Benefits:

- Journaling has been shown to be an effective aid in the treatment of various mental and physical disorders.
- Journaling has been shown to improve the functioning of the immune system. Individuals who journal and write about emotional events tend to be in better overall physical health. For example, a 1999 study in the *Journal of the American Medical Association* documented a 19% improvement in lung function of asthma patients and a 28% improvement in patients with rheumatoid arthritis when they journaled about their emotions.
- Journal therapy has been used as a means of managing grief after tragic events. For example, poetry therapists were enlisted to help students of Columbine High School manage their grief.

- Writing reduces stress because it provides emotional release. Emotional suppression is proven to result in stress, high blood pressure, headaches, weight gain, ulcers and other physical illnesses.

## 2. Historical Benefits:

- Many great writers and ordinary people have contributed to our understanding of the impact of historical events through their journals and diaries. You can impact future generations in your family by chronicling the events taking place in your life and family right now. For example, a pregnancy journal that chronicles the different stages and emotions experienced during the pregnancy can be given to your child at an age of understanding.

- Journals written with this purpose can be a source of wisdom and direction for future generations. Our thought patterns and beliefs affect how we behave in our relationships and what we pass on to those we influence. Sometimes negative thought patterns can affect generations as they are passed on through childrearing philosophies or expressed in the relationship between parent and child.

## 3. Emotional/Spiritual Benefits:

- Writing about our emotions causes our left and right brain hemispheres to work together, allowing emotional and linguistic information to be processed simultaneously. It can help you to communicate and analyze your issues. Though you are delving into your deepest emotions, the act of writing actually creates a sense of detachment. It is believed that this detachment increases the possibility of uncensored expression.

- The two most important relationships that we have in life are with God and self. Though we may have all the trappings of success, we cannot enjoy life without a proper understanding of our individuality. It is easy to lose our identity as we deal with our responsibilities and the various roles we play in life.

Everything you are experiencing today is the result of an issue in your heart, whether it is emotional or spiritual. You are either living the consequences of decisions that came out of your heart, or an external circumstance beyond your control has sparked an issue that was waiting in your heart for the right circumstance to reveal it. This can either be positive or negative. It all depends on what is inside of you.

The heart is the bed of your emotional, spiritual and conceptual life. It is where your affections, desires, joys and perceptions converge. Your heart should be on guard at all times and consciously aware of what is going on in it. We must be careful to not allow words, thoughts and people that are a threat to our emotional health into our hearts. What you allow to enter your heart will manifest in your actions and impact your entire life.

Our thoughts push us in a direction. You cannot think negative thoughts about a person and not begin to distance yourself or mistreat them. You can't lose weight if your mind is consumed with thoughts of cheesecake and chocolate chip cookies. If you think about these things long enough, believe me — you'll give in to them.

Personal development is dependent upon your awareness of your heart. Journaling will help you to make your vision plain. Writing things down produces clarity because it shuts out all the other voices that seem to buzz around in our heads. Writing separates one thought from thousands of distractions. It clears your vision in two ways. First, writing helps you gain a better sense of what you really want. Secondly, it helps you to see things as they really are.

You must make the vision of your life plain by writing it

down. You cannot heal something until you diagnose it. Therefore, writing can help you to develop solutions to the various issues of your life.

## JOURNAL SELECTION

Before you even begin, it is important to find the journal that's right for you. You have to feel comfortable with your journal and feel connected to it. Why? Because we spend more time with the things and people that make us feel comfortable.

- Your journal should be portable. Too many good ideas, moments and inspirations are lost because we fail to write them down. Life lessons are everywhere and you never want to miss the opportunity to capture one when it comes your way. It is like having a friend that always has time for you. If you don't want to carry your journal around, try to keep sheets of loose paper with you that you can store in a binder along with your journal.
- Your journal should reflect your personal style and tastes. Do you want lined or unlined pages? Do you like the way it feels in your hand? Do you like the paper quality? For some, a plain spiral notebook will suffice; others may want more. Journaling is a life-changing practice so approach it with a no-holds-barred attitude.
- Make sure your writing instrument feels comfortable to you as well. You have to enjoy the feel of the pen as it flows across the paper. There's nothing worse than hand cramps when your heart is full and you are caught up in your journaling. Your pen should feel like an extension of your hand.

## JOURNALING TIPS

**Write freely!**

Whatever comes to your mind should end up on your paper. Don't censor your thoughts because in doing so you block the complete development of the process. This isn't grade school; penmanship, spelling and grammar all go out the window. If you feel it, express it. Write as if no one in the world is ever going to see it. Your journal is for you — you are working on getting to know yourself. Don't judge your thoughts as you write them; analysis is for a later time.

**Journal without interruption or distraction.**

Taking time for yourself is crucial to self-care. You need a break from your responsibilities. Spend this time uninterrupted and let your sole focus be on the act of expressing yourself.

**Journal every day!**

Making daily journal entries helps put our thoughts in order. A large portion of our dysfunctions and inability to relate to self and others comes from keeping everything inside in chaos. We are killing ourselves with our silence.

**Date all of your entries.**

This will allow you to easily find whatever entries you may be looking for at a later date. They also serve as a great way of tracking our progress and/or showing us where we still need to grow. Reviewing entries from a year ago can show you a victory that you have overlooked. Or they can show you that what you've been doing hasn't been working and that it's time to develop a new game plan.

## Keep one journal for writing.

Although you can have different types of journals, I highly recommend keeping just one journal where you write about all the different areas of your life. Our lives are not segmented into portions that don't interconnect, but rather one area affects all. I believe you need to see all your thoughts in the context of how they relate one to another. You are trying to get a complete picture of your life.

## Index your journal entries.

Create an index in the last few pages of your journal, so you can keep track of thoughts on certain subjects or events, such as dreams or a particular problem you are working on in your life. This is very helpful when you review your journal entries.

Example: Dreams, April 15, July 22, December 21.

## Keep your journal in a safe place.

The purpose of journaling is defeated if you have to worry about someone else reading what you have written. Buy a combination lock box or store it some place with a key. Peace of mind will help you to journal more freely.

## End each day with gratitude.

End each entry with a list of one or two things for which you are grateful. Gratitude empowers you and will help you to remain focused on your strengths, not your weaknesses. Focusing on what you lack will only serve to breed hopelessness, depression and jealousy in your life.

## JOURNAL REFLECTIONS

### How do I reflect?

You reflect by reviewing what you have written and locating the general theme or pattern that is occurring. Discover the overall mood of what you are saying and try to recall the first thought that sparked that line of thinking. Sometimes our thoughts seem random, but further investigation can reveal how things really relate.

### When do I reflect?

This will depend on how you feel. Sometimes journaling can be such an emotional experience that we just need to close the book and rest afterwards. Exercise your own judgment. However, I do believe it is a good practice to review your entries on a weekly or biweekly basis to help locate yourself emotionally.

### What is my journal telling me about myself?

Our minds are constantly involved in a conversation. We are always thinking, and it is usually when our mind wanders off that we find ourselves in trouble. Because we're so used to the "internal conversations" of our lives, it is easy to tune them out. But we can't afford to ignore these conversations, because they are impacting our behavior and daily lives. The way you see yourself is determining how others treat you and how you interact with life and opportunity. It is also just as important to be in touch with our weaknesses to safeguard ourselves from people and situations that don't bring out the best in us.

## How do I feel about my current situation?

Emotions are not always truth, but they are important. You must examine how you feel because your emotions lead you to the thoughts that you are having about your life. Do you feel that it is hopeless? Have you examined all the possibilities of your situation?

## What are my solutions?

Often in the midst of journaling a problem, we arrive at the solution we need. Sometimes this solution is a plan that can actually be instituted. Sometimes it is merely our recognition that we need to just let go and trust God.

## "AUTHOR YOUR OWN DESTINY!"

## THRIVE! H.E.A.L.I.N.G.™ JOURNALING EXERCISES

### *Help While You're Hurting*

**1. Where can I volunteer?**

_____

_____

_____

_____

_____

_____

_____

_____

_____

_____

_____

_____

> "TO LIVE ONLY FOR YOURSELF IS TO MISS
> THE MEANING AND POWER OF LIFE."

## 2. In what areas are my experiences beneficial to others?

_____

_____

_____

_____

_____

_____

_____

_____

_____

_____

_____

_____

_____

_____

_____

_____

_____

_____

_____

_____

## 3. Who needs me?

> "THE PAIN LETS YOU KNOW
> THAT YOU ARE STILL ALIVE!"

## 4. Where am I hurting?

_____

_____

_____

_____

_____

_____

_____

_____

_____

_____

_____

_____

_____

_____

_____

_____

_____

_____

_____

**5. Who around me is going through a hard time? What can I do to help them?**

_____

_____

_____

_____

_____

_____

_____

_____

_____

_____

_____

_____

_____

_____

_____

_____

_____

_____

_____

_____

_____

_____

_____

> "IF WE FAIL TO DEFINE THE ROLE PAIN
> WILL PLAY IN OUR LIVES, THE PAIN WILL
> REDEFINE US IN ITS IMAGE."

**6. What disappointments have I allowed to define me?**

_____

_____

_____

_____

_____

_____

_____

_____

_____

_____

_____

_____

_____

_____

_____

_____

_____

_____

7. Imagine that you are a mother to someone going through your current experiences. Write a letter to yourself that tells you the things you need to hear.

_____

_____

_____

_____

_____

_____

_____

_____

_____

_____

_____

_____

_____

_____

_____

_____

_____

_____

_____

_____

## *Enjoy Life's Process*

**1. Who do I need to be to attract what I want?**

_____

_____

_____

_____

_____

_____

_____

_____

_____

_____

_____

_____

_____

_____

_____

_____

_____

_____

_____

_____

_____

## 2. What constantly challenges me?

_____

_____

_____

_____

_____

_____

_____

_____

_____

_____

_____

_____

_____

_____

_____

_____

_____

_____

_____

_____

_____

_____

_____

_____

_____

"NO PROGRESS WITHOUT PROCESS."

## 3. What can I do to develop a better attitude?

_____

_____

_____

_____

_____

_____

_____

_____

_____

_____

_____

_____

_____

_____

_____

_____

_____

_____

_____

_____

**4.** What lessons about myself, life and others am I
learning from my current challenges?

_____

_____

_____

_____

_____

_____

_____

_____

_____

_____

_____

_____

_____

_____

_____

_____

_____

_____

_____

_____

_____

_____

"YOUR GRASS CAN BE GREENER—
IF YOU WATER IT!"

**5. What season of my life am I in?**

_____

_____

_____

_____

_____

_____

_____

_____

_____

_____

_____

_____

_____

_____

_____

_____

_____

_____

_____

_____

_____

_____

## 6. What will the next season look like?

_____

_____

_____

_____

_____

_____

_____

_____

_____

_____

_____

_____

_____

_____

_____

_____

_____

_____

_____

_____

_____

_____

_____

_____

_____

## *Accept and Anticipate Change*

**1. As a child, change made me feel...**

_____

_____

_____

_____

_____

_____

_____

_____

_____

_____

_____

_____

_____

_____

_____

_____

_____

_____

_____

_____

_____

_____

**2. What steps of faith can I take to remind myself that I am anticipating a new season?**

_____

_____

_____

_____

_____

_____

_____

_____

_____

_____

_____

_____

_____

_____

_____

_____

_____

_____

_____

_____

_____

_____

_____

_____

_____

> ## "DON'T FEAR CHANGE,
> ## FEAR STAGNATION!"

## 3. What is my attitude towards change?

_____

_____

_____

_____

_____

_____

_____

_____

_____

_____

_____

_____

_____

_____

_____

_____

_____

_____

_____

_____

_____

_____

**4.** Imagine your worst-case scenario. How would you handle it?

_____

_____

_____

_____

_____

_____

_____

_____

_____

_____

_____

_____

_____

_____

_____

_____

_____

_____

_____

_____

_____

_____

_____

_____

_____

> "MEMORIES REHEARSED
> CAN BE MORE POWERFUL THAN
> YOUR PRESENT REALITY."

## 5. What am I afraid to face head on?

_____

_____

_____

_____

_____

_____

_____

_____

_____

_____

_____

_____

_____

_____

_____

_____

_____

_____

_____

## 6. How am I sabotaging my own happiness?

## *Let Go...*

**1. What dead issues/things am I holding on to?**

_____

_____

_____

_____

_____

_____

_____

_____

_____

_____

_____

_____

_____

_____

_____

_____

_____

_____

_____

_____

> "YOU CAN'T STOP WHAT PASSES
> THROUGH YOUR MIND, BUT YOU MUST
> CONTROL WHAT STAYS THERE."

**2.** **What mistakes or pain from my past am I allowing to hinder me in my present relationships?**

_____

_____

_____

_____

_____

_____

_____

_____

_____

_____

_____

_____

_____

_____

_____

_____

_____

_____

_____

3. List your five closest relationships. How do these people
   benefit your life? How do they hinder your growth?

_____

_____

_____

_____

_____

_____

_____

_____

_____

_____

_____

_____

_____

_____

_____

_____

_____

_____

_____

_____

_____

> "THE PROBLEM ISN'T WHAT
> YOU'VE BEEN GETTING. IT'S WHAT
> YOU'VE KEPT!"

4. Name three of the most painful experiences of your life. List what automatically comes to your mind. Have you released them? Have you forgiven all parties involved?

_____

_____

_____

_____

_____

_____

_____

_____

_____

_____

_____

_____

_____

_____

_____

_____

_____

_____

_____

_____

> "FAITH ISN'T ALWAYS STANDING,
> SOMETIMES IT'S A FREE-FALL."

5. What are my comfort zones? What areas do I know I need to change but haven't?

_____

_____

_____

_____

_____

_____

_____

_____

_____

_____

_____

_____

_____

_____

_____

_____

_____

_____

_____

## *Itemize Your Issues and Images*

**1. Who am I? Who have I become out of necessity and as a response to the demands of the world around me?**

_____

_____

_____

_____

_____

_____

_____

_____

_____

_____

_____

_____

_____

_____

_____

_____

_____

_____

_____

_____

_____

_____

**2. Who am I acting for? Who would I like to be?**

_____

_____

_____

_____

_____

_____

_____

_____

_____

_____

_____

_____

_____

_____

_____

_____

_____

_____

_____

_____

_____

_____

## 3. How would my ideal life look?

## 4. What issues in my life am I avoiding?

_____

_____

_____

_____

_____

_____

_____

_____

_____

_____

_____

_____

_____

_____

_____

_____

_____

_____

_____

_____

_____

_____

"IF ANOTHER'S WORDS AND ACTIONS CAN
CAUSE YOU TO REJECT YOUR TRUE SELF,
YOU'VE LET THEM BECOME AN IDOL IN
YOUR LIFE. DON'T BE A REFLECTION,
DARE TO CAST YOUR OWN SHADOW."

5. Who do people say you are? Write a description of yourself from someone else's viewpoint.

"INSECURITY IN SOMEONE ELSE'S
SUCCESS IS A SURE SIGN THAT YOU STILL
DON'T KNOW WHO YOU ARE!"

**6. What am I afraid others will find out about me?**

_____

_____

_____

_____

_____

_____

_____

_____

_____

_____

_____

_____

_____

_____

_____

_____

_____

_____

_____

_____

_____

7. **Clip out pictures from your favorite magazines and newspapers. Choose those things that somehow connect with you. What are these photos telling you about yourself?**

## Navigate Your Needs

**1. Do I feel my needs are legitimate and valid?**

_____

_____

_____

_____

_____

_____

_____

_____

_____

_____

_____

_____

_____

_____

_____

_____

_____

_____

_____

_____

"MORAL CONSISTENCY IN TIMES OF
LACK AND ABUNDANCE IS A TRUE SIGN
OF CHARACTER AND MATURITY."

## 2. How can I help myself?

_____

_____

_____

_____

_____

_____

_____

_____

_____

_____

_____

_____

_____

_____

_____

_____

_____

_____

_____

"MAN'S LOVE HAS CONDITIONS,
BUT GOD'S LOVE HAS NO REASON."

## 3. What do I want from my closest relationships?

_____

_____

_____

_____

_____

_____

_____

_____

_____

_____

_____

_____

_____

_____

_____

_____

_____

_____

_____

_____

_____

## 4. What areas in my life feel out of my control?

**5. What can I do to regain control of my life?**

_____

_____

_____

_____

_____

_____

_____

_____

_____

_____

_____

_____

_____

_____

_____

_____

_____

_____

_____

_____

_____

## 6. Define "Need":

_____

_____

_____

_____

_____

_____

_____

_____

_____

_____

_____

_____

_____

_____

_____

_____

_____

_____

_____

_____

_____

_____

_____

_____

_____

"TO GET WHAT YOU NEED, YOU MUST
GIVE WHAT AND WHEN YOU CAN."

## 7. Define "Desire":

_____

_____

_____

_____

_____

_____

_____

_____

_____

_____

_____

_____

_____

_____

_____

_____

_____

_____

_____

## Grow with Gratitude

**I. What people and things am I grateful for?**

_____

_____

_____

_____

_____

_____

_____

_____

_____

_____

_____

_____

_____

_____

_____

_____

_____

_____

_____

_____

"CHANGE YOUR LIFE
ONE THANK YOU AT A TIME!"

2. Examine your day. What small thing did you overlook that you really are grateful for?

_____

_____

_____

_____

_____

_____

_____

_____

_____

_____

_____

_____

_____

_____

_____

_____

_____

_____

## 3. How is my relationship with God?

"YOU ARE DESTINED TO WIN!
THE QUESTION IS, WILL YOU TAKE
THE JOURNEY?"

**4. What are my strengths?**

_____

_____

_____

_____

_____

_____

_____

_____

_____

_____

_____

_____

_____

_____

_____

_____

**5. Write a letter to your strengths thanking them for getting you through your hard times.**

_____

_____

_____

_____

_____

_____

_____

_____

_____

_____

_____

_____

_____

_____

_____

_____

_____

_____

_____

_____

_____

_____

6. Characterize gratitude as a person. How would he or she look, behave, and respond?

_____

_____

_____

_____

_____

_____

_____

_____

_____

_____

_____

_____

_____

_____

_____

_____

_____

_____

_____

_____

> "PEOPLE WHO OPPOSE YOU AND
> ATTEMPT TO BLOCK YOUR SUCCESS ARE
> JUST FOR WEIGHT LIFTING!"

7. Think of a challenging situation you've recently encountered, and then imagine that you are gratitude. How would you respond?

# PERSONAL DEVELOPMENT
# RESOURCES

*The Holy Bible*
The New International Version (NIV) is my favorite, but find what-
ever version works best for you.

*Understanding Your Potential* by Dr. Myles Munroe
(Shippensburg, PA: Destiny Image, 1996)
This book challenges you to discover your purpose and develop to
your full potential. It is in my opinion a must-read for anyone
who has ever wondered if there is more to life than their present
experience.

*Burden of Freedom* by Dr. Myles Munroe
(Lake Mary, FL: Creation House, 2000)
This is my all-time favorite book by this author. It challenges you
to take responsibility for the kind and quality of life you are living.
Redefining freedom in a whole new light, this book will encourage
you to live the life you dream about.

*Healing for Damaged Emotions* by David Seamands
(Colorado Springs, CO: Chariot Victor Publishing, 1992)
This is not a book of pop psychology, but it is filled with real
answers for real people with real problems. The lights will come on
as you read this one!

*Daddy Loves His Girls* by Bishop TD Jakes
(Lake Mary, FL: Creation House, 1996)
Relationships are what life is all about, and none can deny the
importance of having good relationships with fathers. Written
from a father's perspective, this book reads like a love letter from
the heart of God that will help heal the wounds of the broken and
shattered.

*The Lady, Her Lover & Her Lord* by Bishop TD Jakes
(New York, NY: Penguin Putnam, 1998)
Building on the principles set in motion in *Daddy Loves His Girls*, Bishop Jakes tackles the issues of self-esteem, womanhood and motherhood with sensitivity and insight. I came to an understanding on so many topics while reading this one that I began to take notes in the margins. Needless to say, my copy is now too personal for anyone else to read.

*The Seven Habits of Highly Effective People* by Stephen R. Covey
(New York, NY: Fireside, 1989)
Forget time management, life leadership is what this book is all about. Following the principles in this book will help you focus on what matters to you while ridding you of all the unnecessary extras that eat away at your life and time.

*The On Purpose Person* by Kevin W. McCarthy
(Colorado Springs, CO: Pinon Press, 1992)
If you feel unfulfilled and dissatisfied with your life but don't have much time to spend on reading, this book will do wonders for you. Simple and concise, this book asks the questions that we all need to answer in order to plan our lives.

*The Richest Man in Babylon* by George S. Clason
(New York, NY: Plume, 1957)
The best money book I've ever read. Written in the form of short stories, this gem gives financial principles that will help you gain and keep control of your finances while helping them to grow. Before getting an allowance, every teenager should read this book!

*The Seasons of Life* by Jim Rohn
(Irving, TX: Jim Rohn Productions, 1981)
The beauty of this book is the simplicity with which the author grapples with the different times and seasons of life. In saying the things that we all know but somehow don't grasp, the author has managed to create a thought-provoking and life-changing read.

# Acknowledgments

Thank you, Lord, for the grace and strength you give me to become all that you have destined me to be.

Daddy — Not a day goes by that I don't think of you. I miss your love, I miss your laugh and I miss your smile. Most of all I miss the way you loved me. You are my prince.

Mama — You are my hero! I cannot pay you back for all you have done, but I will spend my life saying thank you. I love you with all my heart.

To my brothers and sisters, I love you all. Jeannie — Through our ups and our downs, thank you for always being there for me. Marc — Thank you for being a source of unending encouragement. You are a true brother, friend and *consigliere*. Wanda — I love you. Real love stands the tests of time and adversity. Gessie — Thank you for being a "true" sister, friend and manager. I could not do it without you. Thank you for the sacrifices you make every day to help make things happen. I can't imagine life without you — so don't go anywhere! Carlos — My little brother, stay hopeful because nothing great happens without hope. The future will only get brighter. Shawna — My boo, you are growing into such a beautiful and powerful young woman. I love you and admire you for having the courage to live your dreams. The world is yours girl!

To my grandparents — Thank you for a legacy of hope and character. You have shown me the value of hard work, discipline and faith in God.

To my nieces and nephews — Auntie loves you. Don't stop until you get to wherever your dreams lead you.

To the Carter family — Thank you for the countless prayers, support and words of encouragement. I look forward to the great things coming your way.

To the Jones family and Tunicia Thompson — Thank you for taking me into your hearts, home and lives. Mommy (Cherral Jones), you are a special and virtuous woman…a rare and precious jewel indeed.

To Scott and Natasha Brown — Thanks for always being there! I am privileged to count you among my family and friends.

To Dr. Myles Munroe and Pastor Ruth Munroe — Thank you for living the message that you teach. As you always say, "See you at the top." I love you and thank you for helping me reveal His glory!

To the Woodstock family — You have come to my rescue at least a thousand times. I appreciate all that you have done to make this book a reality.

To Esther — I'll never forget our times together, and I look forward to years of friendship. Look at what God has done…what a work!

To Mariela — Thanks for always being there. I am proud to have you in my corner and as my friend. Love you much!

To Grafton — Stay focused on your dreams, and remember that each and every setback brings you one step closer to your success. Take care of Gayna, she's a special woman!

To KT — To the oldest young man I've ever met. Can't wait till the world gets a load of your cooking. Don't give up on your vision — it will surely come to pass!

To Sharmayne — You help me get my inside and my outside together. I won't get all mushy because I know you don't like that, but I have to say that I love you and you've touched my life in a special way.

To Cyril and Tryan — You two are the greatest! Thank you for being there for me when no one else was around.

To Walter — Hi Ya Toots! On the road to success, I had to have a "real" job. Thanks for making the trip fun and memorable.

To Ms. Jolley and Mr. and Mrs. Abbott — You are the best teachers I've ever had. You taught me to love learning. I can honestly say that you changed my life.

To the Gebara Family — *Je t'aime de tout mon coeur.*

Special thanks to — Pastor Jacqueline McCullough, The Jermin family, Torie Stewart, Diane Blackman, Reverend Liz Rios and CEFL, Janet Hill, Bertice Berry, Dr. Grace Cornish, Laila Ali, Mike and Regina Henry, Grandma Jean and Grandpa Gaston, Matthew and Debra Gaddy (Matthew, thanks for fixing my computer, I surely couldn't have finished this book without you), Bishop TD Jakes (you inspire me to PUSH beyond the pain), Dinky and Yummy Bingham (you go girl!), Jac Elmers, Allison Warner, Debbie Cowell, Scott Osborne, Fernando Gomez, Stephanie Reichart, Patrik Henry Bass, Imani Powell, Michelle Smith, Cheryl Smith, Patrick Riley, Emma Rogers, Rebecca Wright, Drew Venable, Betty at the NYU Bursar's office (thought I forgot you, but I didn't), Elder George and Minister Ruth Fitzgerald, Clarence Kiu, Roy "Ricky" Rodriguez, Demetrius Frazier (you're alright when you're not making me do sit ups), Lesley Christopher, Daniel Greene, Jon and Christina Meyer, the Doston family, Monica Harris, Ericka Connor, Moira Lindung, Birdie Paul, Aunt Sheila, Sister Betty Elmore, Ms. Ulman (you taught me the beauty of writing and helped take me to another level).

To the literary giants that inspire me and write words that touch generations — Thank you for sharing your gifts with the world: Maya Angelou, Nikki Giovanni, Langston Hughes, Zora Neale Hurston, J. California Cooper, Pablo Neruda and Paul Lawrence Dunbar.

To the friends and family that I failed to mention, charge it to my head and not my heart.

# ORDERING AND CONTACT INFORMATION

Purchase *Thrive! 7 Strategies for Extraordinary Living* one of two ways:

• Bookstores — available in bookstores nationwide through BookWorld Distribution. Visit www.bookworld.com or call 800-444-2524, Ext. 218. BookWorld distributes through all major wholesalers, including Ingram and Baker & Taylor, online retailers such as Amazon.com and services all major chains and independent bookstores.

• Publisher — Call the Butterfly Works office at 718-305-9134 to place your order by phone or visit our website at www.butterflyworks.net.

Our contact information is as follows:

> Butterfly Works
> Post Office Box 5434
> New York, NY 10185
> P: 718-305-9134, F: 718-305-3689
> info@butterflyworks.net
> www.butterflyworks.net

For booking and management:

> The Uplift! Group
> P.O. Box 650518
> Fresh Meadows, NY 11365
> P: 718-591-2447, F: 718-591-1661
> gthompson@upliftgroup.com
> www.upliftgroup.com

Office hours are 9 A.M. — 6 P.M. EST.

# BUTTERFLY
# WORKS

www.butterflyworks.net

**Resources**

**Subscribe** to *Thrive! Today* Felicia T. Scott's FREE monthly newsletter.
(Includes monthly journaling challenges.)

**Shop** for other Felicia T. Scott Books, Audio Books, Seminar Tapes and more!

**Thrive! Seminars**

**See** Felicia T. Scott live at a seminar near you!

**Felicia Scott**

**Schedule** Felicia T. Scott to speak at your:
• Women's, Youth or Singles' Conference
• Personal Development Forum or Empowerment Conference
• Ministry, Book Club or Special Event
• University, High School or Women's Shelter

gthompson@butterflyworks.net
1-718-305-9134

# About the Author

Encouragement Coach Felicia T. Scott communicates her message of extraordinary living with an engaging combination of wit, humor, transparency and straight talk. Scott has been featured in *Essence* Magazine and appeared as a guest on *Good Morning Texas* and *TBN*. She presented her Journal to the Heart of The Matter workshop at the 2002 African American Women on Tour. Her **Thrive! H.E.A.L.I.N.G.™ Seminar** is popular at women's, singles' and youth conferences across the country. A graduate of New York University, the author currently resides in New York City and enjoys speaking to audiences about H.E.A.L.I.N.G.™ and personal development.